# Great Jobs

## *for*

# Music
# Majors

# Great Jobs

## for
# Music
# Majors

*Jan Goldberg*

SERIES DEVELOPERS AND CONTRIBUTING AUTHORS
*Stephen E. Lambert*
*Julie Ann DeGalan*

**VGM Career Horizons**
*NTC/Contemporary Publishing Company*

**Library of Congress Cataloging-in-Publication Data**

Goldberg, Jan.
    Great jobs for music majors / Jan Goldberg.
       p.   cm.
    Includes index.
    ISBN 0-8442-4745-6
    1. Music—Vocational guidance.   2. Job hunting.   3. College
graduates—Employment.   I. Title.
ML3795.G74    1997
780'.23'73—dc21                  97-33295
                                       CIP
                                       MN

Published by VGM Career Horizons
An imprint of NTC/Contemporary Publishing Company
4255 West Touhy Avenue, Lincolnwood (Chicago), Illinois 60646-1975 U.S.A.
Copyright © 1998 by NTC/Contemporary Publishing Company
Printed in the United States of America
International Standard Book Number: 0-8442-4745-6
    17   16   15   14   13   12   11   10   9   8   7   6   5   4   3   2

## Dedication

To my husband, Larry,
for his continual love and support.

To my daughters, Sherri and Debbie,
for always believing in me.

And to the memory of my father and mother,
Sam and Sylvia Lefkovitz, for encouraging me
to follow my dreams.

# CONTENTS

## Acknowledgments

The author gratefully acknowledges the professionals who graciously agreed to be profiled within and all of the associations and organizations that provided valuable and interesting information.

My dear husband, Larry; daughters, Sherri and Debbie; sister Adrienne; and brother, Paul, for their encouragement and support.

Family and close friends Bruce, Michele, Alison, Steven, Marty, Mindi, Cary, Michele, Marci, Steven, Brian, Jesse, Bertha, Aunt Estelle, Uncle Bernard, and Aunt Helen.

A special thanks to a special friend, Diana Catlin.

Sincere gratitude to Betsy Lancefield, Editor, VGM Career Books, for providing this challenging opportunity and help whenever and wherever it is needed.

# MUSIC: A DEGREE FOR ALL GENERATIONS

*Music is well said to be the speech of angels.*

Carlyle, *Essays*

**M**usic has existed for thousands of years. In fact, experts assume that the very first music took the form of chanting by our prehistoric ancestors. Whistles made from the bones of reindeer toes and flutes created from hollow bones have been found dating back to 40,000 years BC.

## ANCIENT AND NOT-SO-ANCIENT HISTORY

In 1400 BC, music was featured at Greek events like funeral ceremonies and feasts. Instruments included pipes and large harps. By 700 BC, music was used in all areas of life in Greece. The word *music,* in fact, is derived from the Greek word *mousike,* which means the arts of music, poetry, and dance. Other musical terms—harmony, orchestra, and guitar—also come from the Greek. Between 400 to 500 BC, Pythagoras used mathematics to define the pitches of the scales of notes still in existence in western music to this day. This was the beginning of writing music in Greece.

In 950, music played an important role in the dedication of King Solomon's temple in Jerusalem. By the year 1000, wandering minstrels were commonly found all over Europe singing songs accompanied by stringed instruments (such as harps) that they played. In 1030, an Italian monk, Guida d'Arezzo created the staff and a system of teaching music which included notes called *ut (do), re, mi, fa, sol, la*. In 1473, the first complete piece of music was printed (rather than handwritten).

The first known composer, the French monk Le'onin, compiled the *Magnus Liber* in 1170. By 1400, towns and royalty like kings, princes, and nobles had their own bands available to play music for social events and ceremonies. In 1637, the first public opera house opened in Venice, Italy, signifying the fact that this form of entertainment began to widen its appeal to the masses. By 1715, the Italian violin maker, Antonio Stradivari (1644–1737), known as Stradivarius, was widely known for his violins, violas, and cellos. (To this date, most feel the richness of their tone has never been surpassed.) In 1742, George Frideric Handel (1685–1759), composed his famous *Messiah*. In 1751, with the addition of two clarinets to an orchestra in Paris, the modern symphony orchestra (including flutes, oboes, clarinets, bassoons, horns, trumpets, and drums) was born.

In 1824, Beethoven arrived at the pinnacle of his career with the performance of his final symphony, no. 9 in D minor A. In 1830, the outstanding Polish composer Frederic Chopin (1810–1849) composed the *Revolutionary Etude*, a piano piece. In 1853, *La Traviata,* composed by Giuseppe Verdi (1813–1901), an Italian composer, was first performed. Verdi went on to compose *Aida* in 1871. Russian Peter Ilyich Tchaikovsky (1840–93) composed his first masterpiece—the *Romeo and Juliet Fantasy Overture*—in 1869. In 1880, he wrote the *1812 Overture* and in 1892, *The Nutcracker*. German composer Johannes Brahms (1833–97) composed *Variations on the St. Anthony Chorale* in 1874. In 1911, Russian composer Igor Stravinsky (1882–1971) wrote the ballet *Petrushka* and in 1913, *The Rite of Spring*. American George Gershwin (1898–1937) wrote the opera *Porgy and Bess* in 1935. Later, Aaron Copland (1990–1990) won a Pulitzer Prize for one of his ballet compositions, *Appalachian Spring*. In 1957, American Leonard Bernstein (1918–1990) composed *West Side Story*.

All of these happenings in music history set the stage for those of you who are today reading this book seeking to make your mark in the field of music. One important ingredient to increase your chances of success lies in preparing yourself.

# THE IMPORTANCE OF EDUCATION

While it is true that having a college degree will not *guarantee* you a position in the world of music (or any other field, for that matter), it is important to realize that this is the best way to prepare yourself and to increase your chances in the job market. No matter what specific career you choose, a higher education will:

1. Offer a broad base of knowledge and experiences

2. Allow you to increase and perfect your skills

3. Provide you with opportunities to gain important personal and professional contacts

4. Give you the information you need to make an informed career decision

Recognizing that there is intense competition out there with a multitude of talented, dedicated people for each job opening, you must always seek to set yourself above and apart from others. A dynamite combination is a college degree with at least one internship, additional formal training or study, and experience working in the field. That's the way to truly position yourself with an edge over other well-qualified candidates.

Good luck in your quest!

# PART ONE

# THE JOB SEARCH

# CHAPTER ONE

# THE SELF-ASSESSMENT

**S**elf-assessment is the process by which you begin to acknowledge your own particular blend of education, experiences, values, needs, and goals. It provides the foundation for career planning and the entire job search process. Self-assessment involves looking inward and asking yourself what can sometimes prove to be difficult questions. This self-examination should lead to an intimate understanding of your personal traits, your personal values, your consumption patterns and economic needs, your longer-term goals, your skill base, your preferred skills, and your underdeveloped skills.

You come to the self-assessment process knowing yourself well in some of these areas, but you may still be uncertain about other aspects. You may be well aware of your consumption patterns, but have you spent much time specifically identifying your longer-term goals, or your personal values as they relate to work? No matter what level of self-assessment you have undertaken to date, it is now time to clarify all of these issues and questions as they relate to the job search.

The knowledge you gain in the self-assessment process will guide the rest of your job search. In this book, you will learn about all of the following tasks:

❑ Writing resumes

❑ Exploring possible job titles

❑ Identifying employment sites

❑ Networking

❑ Interviewing

❑ Following up

❑ Evaluating job offers

In each of these steps, you will rely on and return often to the understanding gained through your self-assessment. Any individual seeking employment must be able and willing to express to potential recruiters and interviewers throughout the job search these facets of his or her personality. This communication allows you to show the world who you are so that together with employers you can determine whether there will be a workable match with a given job or career path.

# How to Conduct a Self-Assessment

The self-assessment process goes on naturally all the time. People ask you to clarify what you mean, or you make a purchasing decision, or you begin a new relationship. You react to the world and the world reacts to you. How you understand these interactions and any changes you might make because of them are part of the natural process of self-discovery. There is, however, a more comprehensive and efficient way to approach self-assessment with regard to employment.

Because self-assessment can become a complex exercise, we have distilled it into a seven-step process that provides an effective basis for undertaking a job search. The seven steps include the following:

1. Understanding your personal traits

2. Identifying your personal values

3. Calculating your economic needs

4. Exploring your longer-term goals

5. Enumerating your skill base

6. Recognizing your preferred skills

7. Assessing skills needing further development

As you work through your self-assessment, you might want to create a worksheet similar to the one shown in Exhibit 1.1. Or you might want to keep a journal of the thoughts you have as you undergo this process. There will be many opportunities to revise your self-assessment as you start down the path of seeking a career.

## STEP 1 Understanding Your Personal Traits

Each person has a unique personality that he or she brings to the job search process. Gaining a better understanding of your personal traits can help you evaluate job and career choices. Identifying these traits, then finding employment that allows you to draw on at least some of them can create a rewarding and fulfilling work experience. If potential employment doesn't allow you to use these preferred traits, it is important to decide whether you can find other ways to express them or

**Exhibit 1.1**

## Self-Assessment Worksheet

**STEP 1.  Understand Your Personal Traits**
The personal traits that describe me are:
*(Include all of the words that describe you.)*


The ten personal traits that most accurately describe me are:
*(List these ten traits.)*


**STEP 2.  Identify Your Personal Values**
Working conditions that are important to me include:
*(List working conditions that would have to exist for you to accept a position.)*


The values that go along with my working conditions are:
*(Write down the values that correspond to each working condition.)*


Some additional values I've decided to include are:
*(List those values you identify as you conduct this job search.)*


**STEP 3.  Calculate Your Economic Needs**
My estimated minimum annual salary requirement is:
*(Write the salary you have calculated based on your budget.)*


Starting salaries for the positions I'm considering are:
*(List the name of each job you are considering and the associated starting salary.)*


**STEP 4.  Explore Your Longer-Term Goals**
My thoughts on longer-term goals right now are:
*(Jot down some of your longer-term goals as you know them right now.)*

continued

continued

**STEP 5. Enumerate Your Skill Base**

The general skills I possess are:
*(List the skills that underlie tasks you are able to complete.)*

The specific skills I possess are:
*(List more technical or specific skills that you possess and indicate your level of expertise.)*

General and specific skills that I want to promote to employers for the jobs I'm considering are:
*(List general and specific skills for each type of job you are considering.)*

**STEP 6. Recognize Your Preferred Skills**

Skills that I would like to use on the job include:
*(List skills that you hope to use on the job, and indicate how often you'd like to use them.)*

**STEP 7. Assess Skills Needing Further Development**

Some skills that I'll need to acquire for the jobs I'm considering include:
*(Write down skills listed in job advertisements or job descriptions that you don't currently possess.)*

I believe I can build these skills by:
*(Describe how you plan to acquire these skills.)*

whether you would be better off not considering this type of job. Interests and hobbies pursued outside of work hours can be one way to use personal traits you don't have an opportunity to draw on in your work. For example, if you consider yourself an outgoing person and the kinds of jobs you are examining allow little contact with other people, you may be able to achieve the level of interaction that is comfortable for you outside of your work setting. If such a compromise seems impractical or otherwise unsatisfactory, you probably should explore only jobs that provide the interaction you want and need on the job.

Many young adults who are not very confident about their attractiveness to employers will downplay their need for income. They will say, "Money is not all that important if I love my work." But if you begin to document exactly what you need for housing, transportation, insurance, clothing, food, and utilities, you will begin to understand that some jobs cannot meet your financial needs and it doesn't matter how wonderful the job is. If you have to worry each payday about bills and other financial obligations, you won't be very effective on the job. Begin now to be honest with yourself about your needs.

**Inventorying Your Personal Traits.** Begin the self-assessment process by creating an inventory of your personal traits. Using the list in Exhibit 1.2, decide which of these personal traits describe you.

---

**Exhibit 1.2**

## Personal Traits

| | | |
|---|---|---|
| Accurate | Critical | Generous |
| Active | Curious | Gentle |
| Adaptable | Daring | Good-natured |
| Adventurous | Decisive | Helpful |
| Affectionate | Deliberate | Honest |
| Aggressive | Detail-oriented | Humorous |
| Ambitious | Determined | Idealistic |
| Analytical | Discreet | Imaginative |
| Appreciative | Dominant | Impersonal |
| Artistic | Eager | Independent |
| Brave | Easygoing | Individualistic |
| Businesslike | Efficient | Industrious |
| Calm | Emotional | Informal |
| Capable | Empathetic | Innovative |
| Caring | Energetic | Intellectual |
| Cautious | Excitable | Intelligent |
| Cheerful | Expressive | Introverted |
| Clean | Extroverted | Intuitive |
| Competent | Fair-minded | Inventive |
| Confident | Farsighted | Jovial |
| Conscientious | Feeling | Just |
| Conservative | Firm | Kind |
| Considerate | Flexible | Liberal |
| Cool | Formal | Likable |
| Cooperative | Friendly | Logical |
| Courageous | Future-oriented | |

continued

continued

| | | |
|---|---|---|
| Loyal | Precise | Serious |
| Mature | Principled | Sincere |
| Methodical | Private | Sociable |
| Meticulous | Productive | Spontaneous |
| Mistrustful | Progressive | Strong |
| Modest | Quick | Strong-minded |
| Motivated | Quiet | Structured |
| Objective | Rational | Subjective |
| Observant | Realistic | Tactful |
| Open-minded | Receptive | Thorough |
| Opportunistic | Reflective | Thoughtful |
| Optimistic | Relaxed | Tolerant |
| Organized | Reliable | Trusting |
| Original | Reserved | Trustworthy |
| Outgoing | Resourceful | Truthful |
| Patient | Responsible | Understanding |
| Peaceable | Reverent | Unexcitable |
| Personable | Sedentary | Uninhibited |
| Persuasive | Self-confident | Verbal |
| Pleasant | Self-controlled | Versatile |
| Poised | Self-disciplined | Wholesome |
| Polite | Sensible | Wise |
| Practical | Sensitive | |

**Focusing on Selected Personal Traits.**   Of all the traits you identified from the list in Exhibit 1.2, select the ten you believe most accurately describe you. If you are having a difficult time deciding, think about which words people who know you well would use to describe you. Keep track of these ten traits.

**Considering Your Personal Traits in the Job Search Process.**   As you begin exploring jobs and careers, watch for matches between your personal traits and the job descriptions you read. Some jobs will require many personal traits you know you possess, and others will not seem to match those traits.

......................................................

Working as a music teacher, for example, will draw upon your reserves of creativity—but not necessarily for your own work. Teaching is essentially outer-directed and your ability to create methods to stimulate, encourage, and guide students will be far more important personal traits for success than your own attention to technique and style. Teaching calls for the ability to motivate others and to support their efforts without being overly critical or judgmental. Music teachers, especially those working within a school system, must be sensitive to the needs and goals of their students, but also be able to work toward meeting the criteria set by others.

...................................................

Your ability to respond to changing conditions, decision-making ability, productivity, creativity, and verbal skills all have a bearing on your success in and enjoyment of your work life. To better guarantee success, be sure to take the time needed to understand these traits in yourself.

## STEP 2   Identifying Your Personal Values

Your personal values affect every aspect of your life, including employment, and they develop and change as you move through life. Values can be defined as principles that we hold in high regard, qualities that are important and desirable to us. Some values aren't ordinarily connected to work (love, beauty, color, light, marriage, family, or religion) and others are (autonomy, cooperation, effectiveness, achievement, knowledge, and security). Our values determine, in part, the level of satisfaction we feel in a particular job.

**Defining Acceptable Working Conditions.**   One facet of employment is the set of working conditions that must exist for someone to consider taking a job.

Each of us would probably create a unique list of acceptable working conditions, but items that might be included on many lists are the amount of money you would need to be paid, how far you are willing to drive or travel, the amount of freedom you want in determining your own schedule, whether you would be working with people or data or things, and the types of tasks you would be willing to do. Your conditions might include statements of working conditions you will *not* accept: for example, you might not be willing to work at night or on weekends or holidays.

If you were offered a job tomorrow, what conditions would have to exist for you to realistically consider accepting the position? Take some time and make a list of these conditions.

**Realizing Associated Values.**   Your list of working conditions can be used to create an inventory of your values relating to jobs and careers you are exploring. For example, if one of your conditions stated that you wanted to earn at least $25,000 per year, the associated value would be financial gain. If another condition was that you wanted to work with a friendly group of people, the value that goes along with that might be belonging or interaction with people. Exhibit 1.3 provides a list of

---

**Exhibit 1.3**

## Work Values

| | | |
|---|---|---|
| Achievement | Development | Physical activity |
| Advancement | Effectiveness | Power |
| Adventure | Excitement | Precision |
| Attainment | Fast pace | Prestige |
| Authority | Financial gain | Privacy |
| Autonomy | Helping | Profit |
| Belonging | Humor | Recognition |
| Challenge | Improvisation | Risk |
| Change | Independence | Security |
| Communication | Influencing others | Self-expression |
| Community | Intellectual stimulation | Solitude |
| Competition | Interaction | Stability |
| Completion | Knowledge | Status |
| Contribution | Leading | Structure |
| Control | Mastery | Supervision |
| Cooperation | Mobility | Surroundings |
| Creativity | Moral fulfillment | Time freedom |
| Decision making | Organization | Variety |

---

commonly held values that relate to the work environment; use it to create your own list of personal values.

**Relating Your Values to the World of Work.** As you read the job descriptions in this book and in other suggested resources, think about the values associated with that position.

····················································

For example, the duties of a music critic would include: listening to recordings, attending performances, and conducting interviews; organizing the information in a logical format; and writing and editing articles and profiles. Associated values are intellectual stimulation, organization, communication, and creativity.

····················································

If you were thinking about a career in this field, or any other field you're exploring, at least some of the associated values should match those you extracted from your list of working conditions. Take a second look at any values that don't match up. How important are they to you? What will happen if they are not satisfied on the job? Can you incorporate those personal values elsewhere? Your answers need to be brutally honest. As you continue your exploration, be sure to add to your list any additional values that occur to you.

## STEP 3  Calculating Your Economic Needs

Each of us grew up in an environment that provided for certain basic needs, such as food and shelter, and, to varying degrees, other needs that we now consider basic, such as cable TV, reading materials, or an automobile. Needs such as privacy, space, and quiet, which at first glance may not appear to be monetary needs, may add to housing expenses and so should be considered as you examine your economic needs. For example, if you place a high value on a large, open living space for yourself, it would be difficult to satisfy that need without an associated high housing cost, especially in a densely populated city environment.

As you prepare to move into the world of work and become responsible for meeting your own basic needs, it is important to consider the salary you will need to be able to afford a satisfying standard of living. The three-step process outlined here will help you plan a budget, which in turn will allow you to evaluate the various career choices and geographic locations you are considering. The steps include (1) developing a realistic budget, (2) examining starting salaries, and (3) using a cost-of-living index.

**Developing a Realistic Budget.**   Each of us has certain expectations for the kind of life-style we want to maintain. In order to begin the process of defining your economic needs, it will be helpful to determine what you expect to spend on routine monthly expenses. These expenses include housing, food, transportation, entertainment, utilities, loan repayments, and revolving charge accounts. A worksheet that details many of these expenses is shown in Exhibit 1.4. You may not currently spend for certain items, but you probably will have to once you begin supporting yourself. As you develop this budget, be generous in your estimates, but keep in mind any items that could be

---

**Exhibit 1.4**

## Estimated Monthly Expenses Worksheet

|  |  | Could Reduce Spending? (Yes/No) |
|---|---|---|
| Cable | $ _____ | _____ |
| Child care | _____ | _____ |
| Clothing | _____ | _____ |

continued

continued

|  | | Could Reduce Spending? (Yes/No) |
|---|---|---|
| Educational loan repayment | _____ | _____ |
| Entertainment | _____ | _____ |
| Food | _____ | _____ |
|   At home | _____ | _____ |
|   Meals out | _____ | _____ |
| Gifts | _____ | _____ |
| Housing | | |
|   Rent/mortgage | _____ | _____ |
|   Insurance | _____ | _____ |
|   Property taxes | _____ | _____ |
| Medical insurance | _____ | _____ |
| Reading materials | | |
|   Newspapers | _____ | _____ |
|   Magazines | _____ | _____ |
|   Books | _____ | _____ |
| Revolving loans/charges | _____ | _____ |
| Savings | _____ | _____ |
| Telephone | _____ | _____ |
| Transportation | | |
|   Auto payment | _____ | _____ |
|   Insurance | _____ | _____ |
|   Parking | _____ | _____ |
| —or | | |
|   Cab/train/bus fare | _____ | _____ |
| Utilities | | |
|   Electric | _____ | _____ |
|   Gas | _____ | _____ |
|   Water/sewer | _____ | _____ |
| Vacations | _____ | _____ |
| Miscellaneous expense 1 | _____ | _____ |
| Expense: _____ | | |
| Miscellaneous expense 2 | _____ | _____ |
| Expense: _____ | | |
| Miscellaneous expense 3 | _____ | _____ |
| Expense: _____ | | |

TOTAL MONTHLY EXPENSES: _____

YEARLY EXPENSES (Monthly expenses x 12): _____

INCREASE TO INCLUDE TAXES (Yearly expenses x 1.35): _____ =
MINIMUM ANNUAL SALARY REQUIREMENT _____

reduced or eliminated. If you are not sure about the cost of a certain item, talk with family or friends who would be able to give you a realistic estimate.

If this is new or difficult for you, start to keep a log of expenses right now. You may be surprised at how much you actually spend each month for food or stamps or magazines. Household expenses and personal grooming items can often loom very large in a budget, as can auto repairs or home maintenance.

Income taxes must also be taken into consideration when examining salary requirements. State and local taxes vary by location, so it is difficult to calculate exactly the effect of taxes on the amount of income you need to generate. To roughly estimate the gross income necessary to generate your minimum annual salary requirement, multiply the minimum salary you have calculated (see Exhibit 1.4) by a factor of 1.35. The resulting figure will be an approximation of what your gross income would need to be, given your estimated expenses.

**Examining Starting Salaries.**   Starting salaries for each of the career tracks are provided throughout this book. These salary figures can be used in conjunction with the cost-of-living index (discussed in the next section) to determine whether you would be able to meet your basic economic needs in a given geographic location.

**Using a Cost-of-Living Index.**   If you are thinking about trying to get a job in a geographic region other than the one where you now live, understanding differences in the cost of living will help you come to a more informed decision about making a move. By using a cost-of-living index, you can compare salaries offered and the cost of living in different locations with what you know about the salaries offered and the cost of living in your present location.

Many variables are used to calculate the cost-of-living index, including housing expenses, groceries, utilities, transportation, health care, clothing, entertainment, local income taxes, and local sales taxes. Cost-of-living indices can be found in many resources, such as *Equal Employment Opportunity Bimonthly, Places Rated Almanac,* or *The Best Towns in America.* They are constantly being recalculated based on changes in costs.

·············································

If you lived in Cleveland, Ohio, for example, and you were interested in working as a staff music critic for the *Cleveland Plain Dealer,* you would earn, on average, $26,643 annually. But let's say you're also thinking about moving to either New York, Los Angeles, or Minneapolis. You know you can live on $26,643 in Cleveland, but you want to be able to equal that salary in the other locations you're considering. How much will you need to earn in those locations to do this? Figuring the cost of living for each city will show you.

Let's walk through this example. In any cost-of-living index, the number 100 represents the national average cost of living, and each city is assigned an index number based on current prices in that city for the items included in the index (housing, food, etc.). In the index we used, New York was assigned the number 213.3, Los Angeles's index was 124.6, Minneapolis's was 100.0, and Cleveland's index was 114.3. In other words, it costs more than twice as much to live in New York as it does in Minneapolis. We can set up a table to determine exactly how much you would have to earn in each of these cities to have the same buying power that you have in Cleveland.

**Job: Sales Representative**

| CITY | INDEX | EQUIVALENT SALARY |
|------|-------|-------------------|
| $\dfrac{\text{New York}}{\text{Cleveland}}$ | $\dfrac{213.3}{114.3}$ | x \$26,643 = \$49,720 in New York |
| $\dfrac{\text{Los Angeles}}{\text{Cleveland}}$ | $\dfrac{124.6}{114.3}$ | x \$26,643 = \$29,044 in Los Angeles |
| $\dfrac{\text{Minneapolis}}{\text{Cleveland}}$ | $\dfrac{100.0}{114.3}$ | x \$26,643 = \$24,382 in Minneapolis |

You would have to earn \$49,720 in New York, \$29,044 in Los Angeles, and \$24,382 in Minneapolis to match the buying power of \$26,643 in Cleveland.

If you would like to determine whether it's financially worthwhile to make any of these moves, one more piece of information is needed: the salaries of music critics in these other cities. The *Dow Jones Newspaper Fund* reports the following average salary information for newspaper staff as of 1994:

| Newspaper | Annual Salary | Salary Equivalent to Ohio | Change in Buying Power |
|---|---|---|---|
| New York Times | $60,266 | $49,720 | +$10,546 |
| Los Angeles Daily News | $24,700 | $29,044 | –$ 4,344 |
| Minneapolis Star Tribune | $23,244 | $24,382 | –$ 1,138 |
| Cleveland Plain Dealer | $26,643 | — | — |

> If you moved to New York City and secured employment as a music critic at the *New York Times,* you would be able to maintain a lifestyle similar to the one you led in Cleveland; in fact, you would even be able to enhance your lifestyle given the increase in buying power. The same would not be true for a move to Los Angeles or Minneapolis. You would decrease your buying power given the rate of pay and cost of living in these cities.

You can work through a similar exercise for any type of job you are considering and for many locations when current salary information is available. It will be worth your time to undertake this analysis if you are seriously considering a relocation. By doing so you will be able to make an informed choice.

## STEP 4   Exploring Your Longer-Term Goals

There is no question that when we first begin working, our goals are to use our skills and education in a job that will reward us with employment, income, and status relative to the preparation we brought with us to this position. If we are not being paid as much as we feel we should for our level of education, or if job demands don't provide the intellectual stimulation we had hoped for, we experience unhappiness and, as a result, often seek other employment.

Most jobs we consider "good" are those that fulfill our basic "lower-level" needs of security, food, clothing, shelter, income, and productive work. But even when our basic needs are met and our jobs are secure and productive, we as individuals are constantly changing. As we change, the demands and expectations we place on our jobs may change. Fortunately, some jobs grow and change with us, and this explains why some people are happy throughout many years in a job.

But more often people are bigger than the jobs they fill. We have more goals and needs than any job could fulfill. These are "higher-level" needs of self-esteem, companionship, affection, and an increasing desire to feel we are employing our-selves in the most effective way possible. Not all of these higher-level needs can be fulfilled through employment, but for as long as we are employed, we increasingly demand that our jobs play their part in moving us along the path to fulfillment.

Another obvious but important fact is that we change as we mature. Although our jobs also have the potential for change, they may not change as frequently or as markedly as we do. There are increasingly fewer one-job, one-employer careers; we must think about a work future that may involve voluntary or forced moves from employer to employer. Because of that very real possibility, we need to take advan-tage of the opportunities in each position we hold to acquire skills and competen-cies that will keep us viable and attractive as employees in a job market that is not only increasingly technology/computer dependent, but also is populated with more and more small, self-transforming organizations rather than the large, seem-ingly stable organizations of the past.

It may be difficult in the early stages of the job search to determine wheth-er the path you are considering can meet these longer-term goals. Reading about career paths and individual career histories in your field can be very helpful in this regard. Meeting and talking with individuals further along in their careers can be enlightening as well. Older workers can provide valuable guidance on "self-managing" your career, which will become an increasingly valuable skill in the future. Some of these ideas may seem remote as you read this now, but you should be able to appreciate the need to ensure that you are growing, developing valuable new skills, and researching other employers who might be interested in your particular skills package.

· · · · · · · · · · · · · · · · · · · · · · · · · · · · · · · · · · · · · ·

**If you are considering a career as a music teacher, you would gain a better perspective on this path if you talked to teachers working in different settings: a music teacher working with private students; one working within the public school system; another at the university level or with a private music institute. Each will have a different perspective, unique concerns, and an individual set of value priorities.**

· · · · · · · · · · · · · · · · · · · · · · · · · · · · · · · · · · · · · ·

## STEP 5  Enumerating Your Skill Base

In terms of the job search, skills can be thought of as capabilities that can be devel-oped in school, at work, or by volunteering and then used in specific job settings. Many studies have documented the kinds of skills that employers seek in entry-level applicants. For example, some of the most desired skills for individuals interested in the teaching profession include the ability to interact effectively with students one on one, to manage a classroom, to adapt to varying situations as necessary, and to get involved in school activities. Business employers have also identified important qualities, including enthusiasm for the employer's product or service, a businesslike mind, the ability to follow written or verbal instructions, the ability to demonstrate self-control, the confidence to suggest new ideas, the ability to communicate with all members of a group, awareness of cultural differences, and loyalty, to name just a few. You will find that many of these skills are also in the repertoire of qualities demanded in your college major.

In order to be successful in obtaining any given job, you must be able to demonstrate that you possess a certain mix of skills that will allow you to carry out the duties required by that job. This skill mix will vary a great deal from job to job; to determine the skills necessary for the jobs you are seeking, you can read job advertisements or more generic job descriptions, such as those found later in this book. If you want to be effective in the job search, you must directly show employers that you possess the skills needed to be successful in filling the position. These skills will initially be described on your resume and then discussed again during the interview process.

Skills are either general or specific. General skills are those that are developed throughout the college years by taking classes, being employed, and getting involved in other related activities such as volunteer work or campus organizations. General skills include the ability to read and write, to perform computations, to think critically, and to communicate effectively. Specific skills are also acquired on the job and in the classroom, but they allow you to complete tasks that require specialized knowledge. Computer programming, drafting, language translating, and copy editing are just a few examples of specific skills that may relate to a given job.

In order to develop a list of skills relevant to employers, you must first identify the general skills you possess, then list specific skills you have to offer, and, finally, examine which of these skills employers are seeking.

**Identifying Your General Skills.**  Because you possess or will possess a college degree, employers will assume that you can read and write, perform certain basic computations, think critically, and communicate effectively. Employers will want to see that you have acquired these skills, and they will want to know which additional general skills you possess.

One way to begin identifying skills is to write an experiential diary. An experiential diary lists all the tasks you were responsible for completing for each job you've held and then outlines the skills required to do those tasks. You may list several skills for any given task. This diary allows you to distinguish between the tasks you performed and the underlying skills required to complete those tasks. Here's an example:

| Tasks | Skills |
|---|---|
| Answering telephone | Effective use of language, clear diction, ability to direct inquiries, ability to solve problems |
| Waiting on tables | Poise under conditions of time and pressure, speed, accuracy, good memory, simultaneous completion of tasks, sales skills |

For each job or experience you have participated in, develop a worksheet based on the example shown here. On a resume, you may want to describe these skills rather than simply listing tasks. Skills are easier for the employer to appreciate, especially when your experience is very different from the employment you are seeking. In addition to helping you identify general skills, this experiential diary will prepare you to speak more effectively in an interview about the qualifications you possess.

**Identifying Your Specific Skills.**   It may be easier to identify your specific skills, because you can definitely say whether you can speak other languages, program a computer, draft a map or diagram, or edit a document using appropriate symbols and terminology.

Using your experiential diary, identify the points in your history where you learned how to do something very specific, and decide whether you have a beginning, intermediate, or advanced knowledge of how to use that particular skill. Right now, be sure to list *every* specific skill you have, and don't consider whether you like using the skill. Write down a list of specific skills you have acquired and the level of competence you possess—beginning, intermediate, or advanced.

**Relating Your Skills to Employers.**   You probably have thought about a couple of different jobs you might be interested in obtaining, and one way to begin relating the general and specific skills you possess to potential employer needs is to read actual advertisements for these types of positions (see Part II for resources listing actual job openings).

..................................................

For example, you might be interested in a career as an orchestra conductor. A typical job listing might read, "Requires 2–5 years experience, professional expertise, interpersonal skills, creativity, drive, and the ability to work under pressure." If you then used any one of a number of general sources of information that describe the job of an orchestra conductor, you would find additional information. Conductors also audition and select musicians, choose the music to accommodate the talents and the abilities of the musicians, direct rehearsals, and conduct the performances.

Begin building a comprehensive list of required skills with the first job description you read. Exploring advertisements for and descriptions of several types of related positions will reveal an important core of skills necessary for obtaining the type of work you're interested in. In building this list, include both general and specific skills.

Following is a sample list of skills needed to be a successful orchestra conductor. On the left, you'll find the general skills most useful for conducting an orchestra. On the right are specific skills related to on-the-job tasks. These items were extracted from general resources and actual job listings.

---

**Job: Orchestra Conductor**

| General Skills | Specific Skills |
|---|---|
| Work in noisy environment | Develop creative programs |
| Work long hours near deadline | Assign seating |
| Work well with other people | Select specific musical arrangements |
| Exhibit talent | Schedule auditions |
| Be organized | Hire musicians |
| Be able to supervise the work of others | Schedule and direct rehearsals |
| Have a specific body of knowledge | Conduct performances |

---

On separate sheets of paper, try to generate a comprehensive list of required skills for at least one job you are considering.

The list of general skills that you develop for a given career path would be valuable for any number of jobs you might apply for. Many of the specific skills would also be transferable to other types of positions. For example, orchestra conductors audition and select musicians based on the current needs of the orchestra. Choral directors would perform similar duties and possess similar skills to audition and select singers for glee clubs or choirs.

......................................................

Now review the list of skills you developed and check off those skills that *you know you possess* and that are required for jobs you are considering. You should refer to these specific skills on the resume that you write for this type of job. See Chapter 2 for details on resume writing.

## STEP 6  Recognizing Your Preferred Skills

In the previous section, you developed a comprehensive list of skills that relate to particular career paths that are of interest to you. You can now relate these to skills that you prefer to use. We all use a wide range of skills (some researchers say individuals have a repertoire of about 500 skills), but we may not be particularly interested in using all of them in our work. There may be some skills that come to us more naturally or that we use successfully time and time again and that we want to continue to use; these are best described as our preferred skills. For this exercise, use the list of skills that you developed for the previous section and decide which of them you are *most interested in using* in future work and how often you would like to use them. You might be interested in using some skills only occasionally, while others you would like to use more regularly. You probably also have skills that you hope you can use constantly.

As you examine job announcements, look for matches between this list of preferred skills and the qualifications described in the advertisements. These skills should be highlighted on your resume and discussed in job interviews.

## STEP 7  Assessing Skills Needing Further Development

Previously you developed a list of general and specific skills required for given positions. You already possess some of these skills; those that remain to be developed are your underdeveloped skills.

If you are just beginning the job search, there may be gaps between the qualifications required for some of the jobs being considered and skills you possess. These are your underdeveloped skills. The thought of having to admit to and talk about these underdeveloped skills, especially in a job interview, is a frightening one. One way to put a healthy perspective on this subject is to target and relate your exploration of underdeveloped skills to the types of positions you are seeking. Recognizing these shortcomings and planning to overcome them with either on-the-job training or additional formal education can be a positive way to address the concept of underdeveloped skills.

On your worksheet or in your journal, make a list of up to five general or specific skills required for the positions you're interested in that you *don't currently possess.* For each item, list an idea you have for specific action you could take to acquire that skill. Do some brainstorming to come up with possible actions. If you have a hard time generating ideas, talk to people currently working in this type of position, professionals in your college career services office, trusted friends, family members, or members of related professional associations.

If, for example, you are interested in a job for which you don't have some specific required experience, you could locate training opportunities such as classes or workshops offered through a local college or university, community college, or club or association that would help you build the level of expertise you need for the job.

You might have noticed in this book that many excellent positions for your major demand computer skills. These computer skills were probably not part of your required academic preparation. While it is easy for the business world to see the direct link between oral and written communication and high technology, some college departments have been markedly reluctant to add this dimension to their curriculums. What can you do now? If you're still in college, take what computer courses you can before you graduate. If you've already graduated, look at evening programs, continuing education courses, or tutorial programs that may be available commercially. Developing a modest level of expertise will encourage you to be more confident in suggesting to potential employers that you can continue to add to your skill base on the job.

In Chapter 5 on interviewing, we will discuss in detail how to effectively address questions about underdeveloped skills. Generally speaking, though, employers want genuine answers to these types of questions. They want you to reveal "the real you," and they also want to see how you answer difficult questions. In taking the positive, targeted approach discussed above, you show the employer that you are willing to continue to learn and that you have a plan for strengthening your job qualifications.

## USING YOUR SELF-ASSESSMENT

Exploring entry-level career options can be an exciting experience if you have good resources available and will take the time to use them. Can you effectively complete the following tasks?

1. Understand and relate your personality traits to career choices

2. Define your personal values

3. Determine your economic needs

4. Explore longer-term goals

5. Understand your skill base

6. Recognize your preferred skills

7. Express a willingness to improve on your underdeveloped skills

If so, then you can more meaningfully participate in the job search process by writing a more effective resume, finding job titles that represent work you are interested in doing, locating job sites that will provide the opportunity for you to use your strengths and skills, networking in an informed way, participating in focused interviews, getting the most out of follow-up contacts, and evaluating job offers to find those that create a good match between you and the employer. The remaining chapters guide you through these next steps in the job search process. For many job seekers, this process can take anywhere from three months to a year to implement. The time you will need to put into your job search will depend on the type of job you want and the geographic location where you'd like to work. Think of your effort as a job in itself, requiring you to set aside time each week to complete the needed work. Carefully undertaken efforts may reduce the time you need for your job search.

# CHAPTER TWO

# THE RESUME AND COVER LETTER

T he task of writing a resume may seem overwhelming if you are unfamiliar with this type of document, but there are some easily understood techniques that can and should be used. This section was written to help you understand the purpose of the resume, the different types of resume formats available, and how to write the sections of information traditionally found on a resume. We will present examples and explanations that address questions frequently posed by people writing their first resume or updating an old resume.

Even within the formats and suggestions given below, however, there are infinite variations. True, most resumes follow one of the outlines suggested below, but you should feel free to adjust the resume to suit your needs and make it expressive of your life and experience.

## WHY WRITE A RESUME?

The purpose of a resume is to convince an employer that you should be interviewed. You'll want to present enough information to show that you can make an immediate and valuable contribution to an organization. A resume is not an in-depth historical or legal document; later in the job search process you'll be asked to document your entire work history on an application form and attest to its validity. The resume should, instead, highlight relevant information pertaining directly to the organization that will receive the document or the type of position you are seeking.

We will discuss four types of resumes in this chapter: chronological resume, functional resume, targeted resume, and the broadcast letter. The reasons for using one type of resume over another and the typical format for each are addressed in the following sections.

# The Chronological Resume

The chronological resume is the most common of the various resume formats and therefore the format that employers are most used to receiving. This type of resume is easy to read and understand because it details the chronological progression of jobs you have held. (See Exhibit 2.1.) It begins with your most recent employment and works back in time. If you have a solid work history, or experience that provided growth and development in your duties and responsibilities, a chronological resume will highlight these achievements. The typical elements of a chronological resume include the heading, a career objective, educational background, employment experience, activities, and references.

## The Heading
The heading consists of your name, address, and telephone number. Recently it has come to include fax numbers and electronic mail addresses as well. We suggest that you spell out your full name and type it in all capital letters in bold type. After all, *you* are the focus of the resume! If you have a current as well as a permanent address and you include both in the heading, be sure to indicate until what date your current address will be valid. The two-letter state abbreviation should be the only abbreviation that appears in your heading. Don't forget to include the zip code with your address and the area code with your telephone number.

## The Objective
As you formulate the wording for this part of your resume, keep the following points in mind.

**The Objective Focuses the Resume.** Without a doubt, this is the most challenging part of the resume for most resume writers. Even for individuals who have quite firmly decided on a career path, it can be difficult to encapsulate all they want to say in one or two brief sentences. For job seekers who are unfocused or unclear about their intentions, trying to write this section can inhibit the entire resume writing process.

Recruiters tell us, time and again, that the objective creates a frame of reference for them. It helps them see how you express your goals and career focus. In

**Exhibit 2.1**

## Chronological Resume

### JILL GOLDMAN

323 Gainesborough Street
Boston, MA 02122
(617) 555-8841
(until June 1997)

75 First Street
Pelham, NH 03076
(603) 555-2030

### OBJECTIVE

A career as a music therapist in a hospital or other health care facility, ultimately moving into a supervisory position.

### EDUCATION

Bachelor of Science
Double Major: Occupational Therapy and Music
Northeastern University
Boston, Massachusetts
June 1997

### RELATED COURSES

| | |
|---|---|
| Child Development | Abnormal Psychology |
| Music History | Business of Music |
| Health Care Management | Kinesiology |

### EXPERIENCE

**Internships**                                        1996 to 1997
Newton–Wellesley Hospital, Newton, Massachusetts
Beth Israel Hospital, Brookline, Massachusetts
Veterans Hospital, Boston, Massachusetts
Nine-month internship rotating through various facilities and working with a variety of patients including stroke victims and amputees.

**Part-time Tutoring**                                        1993 to 1997
Piano and Voice Lessons
Throughout my four years of college I have given weekly piano and voice lessons to a variety of private students.

continued

continued

**Summer Work**                                              1994 and 1995
Camp Sa–Gis–Ca
Acton, Maine
Camp counselor for two summers at an overnight Girl Scout camp.

### COMMUNITY SERVICE
Volunteer, Big Brothers/Big Sisters, Boston, Massachusetts
Acted as Big Sister to a 12-year-old.
Fund-raising, American Red Cross, Boston, Massachusetts

### REFERENCES
Both personal and professional references are available upon request.

addition, the statement may indicate in what ways you can immediately benefit an organization. Given the importance of the objective, every point covered in the resume should relate to it. If information doesn't relate, it should be omitted. With the word processing technology available today, each resume can and should be tailored for individual employers or specific positions that are available.

**Choose an Appropriate Length.**   Because of the brevity necessary for a resume, you should keep the objective as short as possible. Although objectives of only four or five words often don't show much direction, objectives that take three full lines would be viewed as too wordy and might possibly be ignored.

**Consider Which Type of Objective Statement You Will Use.**   There are many ways to state an objective, but generally there are four forms this statement can take: (1) a very general statement; (2) a statement focused on a specific position; (3) a statement focused on a specific industry; or (4) a summary of your qualifications. In our contacts with employers, we often hear that many resumes don't exhibit any direction or career goals, so we suggest avoiding general statements when possible.

*1. General Objective Statement.*   General objective statements look like the following:

- ❑ An entry-level educational programming coordinator position

- ❑ An entry-level marketing position

This type of objective would be useful if you know what type of job you want but you're not sure which industries interest you.

**2. *Position-Focused Objective.*** Following are examples of objectives focusing on a specific position:

❑ To obtain the position of Conference Coordinator at State College

❑ To obtain a position as Assistant Editor at *Time* magazine

When a student applies for an advertised job opening, this type of focus can be very effective. The employer knows that the applicant has taken the time to tailor the resume specifically for this position.

**3. *Industry-Focused Objective.*** Focusing on a particular industry in an objective could be stated as follows:

❑ To begin a career as a sales representative in the cruise line industry

**4. *Summary of Qualifications Statement.*** The summary of qualifications can be used instead of an objective or in conjunction with an objective. The purpose of this type of statement is to highlight relevant qualifications gained through a variety of experiences. This type of statement is often used by individuals with extensive and diversified work experience. An example of a qualifications statement follows:

········································

A degree in music education and one year of experience in an elementary school as a student music teacher have prepared me for a career as a full-time music teacher in an educational institution that values hands-on involvement and creativity.

········································

**Support Your Objective.** A resume that contains any one of these types of objective statements should then go on to demonstrate why you are qualified to get the position. Listing academic degrees can be one way to indicate qualifications. Another demonstration would be in the way previous experiences, both volunteer and paid, are described. Without this kind of documentation in the body of the resume, the objective looks unsupported. Think of the resume as telling a connected story about you. All the elements should work together to form a coherent picture that ideally should relate to your statement of objective.

## Education

This section of your resume should indicate the exact name of the degree you will receive or have received, spelled out completely with no abbreviations.

The degree is generally listed after the objective, followed by the institution name and address, and then the month and year of graduation. This section could also include your academic minor, grade point average (GPA), and appearance on the Dean's List or President's List.

If you have enough space, you might want to include a section listing courses related to the field in which you are seeking work. The best use of a "related courses" section would be to list some course work that is not traditionally associated with the major. Perhaps you took several computer courses outside your degree that will be helpful and related to the job prospects you are entertaining. Several education section examples are shown here:

········································

❑ Bachelor of Arts Degree in Music
Boston University, Boston, Massachusetts, May 1997
Minor: Psychology

❑ Bachelor of Arts Degree in Music Education
Tufts University, Medford, Massachusetts, May 1997
Minor: Drama

❑ Bachelor of Arts Degree in Music
State University, Boulder, Colorado, June 1997
Minor: English

An example of a format for a related-courses section follows:

| RELATED COURSES | |
| --- | --- |
| Educational Administration | Creative Writing |
| Economics | Technical Writing |
| Desktop Publishing | Computer Graphics |

········································

## Experience

The experience section of your resume should be the most substantial part and should take up most of the space on the page. Employers want to see what kind of work history you have. They will look at your range of experiences, longevity in jobs, and specific tasks you are able to complete. This section may also be called "work experience," "related experience," "employment history," or "employment." No matter what you call this section, some important points to remember are the following:

1. **Describe your duties** as they relate to the position you are seeking.

2. **Emphasize major responsibilities** and indicate increases in responsibility. Include all relevant employment experiences: summer, part-time, internships, cooperative education, or self-employment.

3. **Emphasize skills,** especially those that transfer from one situation to another. The fact that you coordinated a student organization, chaired meetings, supervised others, and managed a budget leads one to suspect that you could coordinate other things as well.

4. **Use descriptive job titles** that provide information about what you did. A "Student Intern" should be more specifically stated as, for example, "Magazine Operations Intern." "Volunteer" is also too general; a title like "Peer Writing Tutor" would be more appropriate.

5. **Create word pictures** by using active verbs to start sentences. Describe *results* you have produced in the work you have done.

A limp description would say something like the following: "My duties included helping with production, proofreading, and editing. I used a word processing package to alter text." An action statement would be stated as follows: "Coordinated and assisted in the creative marketing of brochures and seminar promotions, becoming proficient in WordPerfect."

Remember, an accomplishment is simply a result, a final measurable product that people can relate to. A duty is not a result, it is an obligation—every job holder has duties. For an effective resume, list as many results as you can. To make the most of the limited space you have and to give your description impact, carefully select appropriate and accurate descriptors from the list of action words in Exhibit 2.2.

---

**Exhibit 2.2**

## Resume Action Verbs

| | | |
|---|---|---|
| Achieved | Collected | Converted |
| Acted | Communicated | Coordinated |
| Administered | Compiled | Corrected |
| Advised | Completed | Created |
| Analyzed | Composed | Decreased |
| Assessed | Conceptualized | Defined |
| Assisted | Condensed | Demonstrated |
| Attained | Conducted | Designed |
| Balanced | Consolidated | Determined |
| Budgeted | Constructed | Developed |
| Calculated | Controlled | Directed |

continued

continued

| | | |
|---|---|---|
| Documented | Learned | Received |
| Drafted | Lectured | Recommended |
| Edited | Led | Recorded |
| Eliminated | Maintained | Reduced |
| Ensured | Managed | Reinforced |
| Established | Mapped | Reported |
| Estimated | Marketed | Represented |
| Evaluated | Met | Researched |
| Examined | Modified | Resolved |
| Explained | Monitored | Reviewed |
| Facilitated | Negotiated | Scheduled |
| Finalized | Observed | Selected |
| Generated | Obtained | Served |
| Handled | Operated | Showed |
| Headed | Organized | Simplified |
| Helped | Participated | Sketched |
| Identified | Performed | Sold |
| Illustrated | Planned | Solved |
| Implemented | Predicted | Staffed |
| Improved | Prepared | Streamlined |
| Increased | Presented | Studied |
| Influenced | Processed | Submitted |
| Informed | Produced | Summarized |
| Initiated | Projected | Systematized |
| Innovated | Proposed | Tabulated |
| Instituted | Provided | Tested |
| Instructed | Qualified | Transacted |
| Integrated | Quantified | Updated |
| Interpreted | Questioned | Verified |
| Introduced | Realized | |

Here are some traits that employers tell us they like to see:

❑ Teamwork

❑ Energy and motivation

❑ Learning and using new skills

❑ Demonstrated versatility

❑ Critical thinking

❑ Understanding how profits are created

❑ Displaying organizational acumen

- Communicating directly and clearly, in both writing and speaking
- Risk taking
- Willingness to admit mistakes
- Manifesting high personal standards

# SOLUTIONS TO FREQUENTLY ENCOUNTERED PROBLEMS

## Repetitive Employment with the Same Employer

EMPLOYMENT: **The Foot Locker,** Portland, Oregon. Summer 1991, 1992, 1993. Initially employed in high school as salesclerk. Due to successful performance, asked to return next two summers at higher pay with added responsibility. Ranked as the #2 salesperson the first summer and #1 the next two summers. Assisted in arranging eye-catching retail displays; served as manager of other summer workers during owner's absence.

## A Large Number of Jobs

EMPLOYMENT: Recent Hospitality Industry Experience: Affiliated with four upscale hotel/restaurant complexes (September 1991–February 1994), where I worked part- and full-time as a waiter, bartender, disc jockey, and bookkeeper to produce income for college.

## Several Positions with the Same Employer

EMPLOYMENT: Coca-Cola Bottling Co., Burlington, VT, 1991–94. In four years, I received three promotions, each with increased pay and responsibility.

Summer Sales Coordinator: Promoted to hire, train, and direct efforts of add-on staff of 15 college-age route salespeople hired to meet summer peak demand for product.

Sales Administrator: Promoted to run home office sales desk, managing accounts and associated delivery schedules for professional sales force of ten people. Intensive phone work, daily interaction with all personnel, and strong knowledge of product line required.

Route Salesperson: Summer employment to travel and tourism industry sites using Coke products. Met specific schedule demands, used good communication skills with wide variety of customers, and demonstrated strong selling skills. Named salesperson of the month for July and August of that year.

# Questions Resume Writers Often Ask

## How Far Back Should I Go in Terms of Listing Past Jobs?

Usually, listing three or four jobs should suffice. If you did something back in high school that has a bearing on your future aspirations for employment, by all means list the job. As you progress through your college career, high school jobs may be replaced on the resume by college employment.

## Should I Differentiate between Paid and Nonpaid Employment?

Most employers are not initially as concerned about how much you were paid. They are anxious to know how much responsibility you held in your past employment. There is no need to specify that your work was volunteer if you had significant responsibilities.

## How Should I Represent My Accomplishments or Work-Related Responsibilities?

Succinctly, but fully. In other words, give the employer enough information to arouse curiosity, but not so much detail that you leave nothing to the imagination. Besides, some jobs merit more lengthy explanations than others. Be sure to convey any information that can give an employer a better understanding of the depth of your involvement at work. Did you supervise others? How many? Did your efforts result in a more efficient operation? How much did you increase efficiency? Did you handle a budget? How much? Were you promoted in a short time? Did you work two jobs at once or 15 hours per week after high school? Where appropriate, quantify.

## Should the Work Section Always Follow the Education Section on the Resume?

Always lead with your strengths. If your past work closely relates to the employment you now seek, put this section after the objective. Or, if you are weak on the academic side but have a surplus of good work experiences, consider reversing the order of your sections to lead with employment, followed by education.

## How Should I Present My Activities, Honors, Awards, Professional Societies, and Affiliations?

This section of the resume can add valuable information for an employer to consider if used correctly. The rule of thumb for information in this section is to include only those activities that are in some way relevant to the objective stated on your resume. If you can draw a valid connection between your activities and your objective, include them; if not, leave them out.

Granted, this is hard to do. Center on the championship basketball team or coordinator of the biggest homecoming parade ever held are roles that have meaning for you and represent personal accomplishments you'd like to share. But the resume is a brief document, and the information you provide on it should help the employer make a decision about your job eligibility. Including personal details can be confusing and could hurt your candidacy. Limiting your activity list to a few very significant experiences can be very effective.

If you are applying for a position as a safety officer, your certificate in Red Cross lifesaving skills or CPR would be related and valuable. You would want to include it. If, however, you are applying for a job as a junior account executive in an advertising agency, that information would be unrelated and superfluous. Leave it out.

Professional affiliations and honors should *all* be listed; especially important are those related to your job objective. Social clubs and activities need not be a part of your resume unless you hold a significant office or you are looking for a position related to your membership. Be aware that most prospective employers' principle concerns are related to your employability, not your social life. If you have any, publications can be included as an addendum to your resume.

The focus of the resume is your experience and education. It is not necessary to describe your involvement in activities. However, if your resume needs to be lengthened, this section provides the freedom either to expand on or mention only briefly the contributions you have made. If you have made significant contributions (e.g., an officer of an organization or a particularly long tenure with a group), you may choose to describe them in more detail. It is not always necessary to include the dates of your memberships with your activities the way you would include job dates.

There are a number of different ways in which to present additional information. You may give this section a number of different titles. Assess what you want to list, and then use an appropriate title. Do not use extracurricular activities. This terminology is scholastic, not professional, and therefore not appropriate. The following are two examples:

❑ ACTIVITIES:  Society for Technical Communication, Student Senate, Student Admissions Representative, Senior Class Officer

❑ ACTIVITIES:  • Society for Technical Communication Member
  • Student Senator
  • Student Admissions Representative
  • Senior Class Officer

The position you are looking for will determine what you should or should not include. *Always* look for a correlation between the activity and the prospective job.

## How Should I Handle References?

The use of references is considered a part of the interview process, and they should never be listed on a resume. You would always provide references to a potential employer if requested to, so it is not even necessary to include this section on the resume if room does not permit. If space is available, it is acceptable to include one of the following statements:

- ❏ REFERENCES: Furnished upon request.

- ❏ REFERENCES: Available upon request.

Individuals used as references must be protected from unnecessary contacts. By including names on your resume, you leave your references unprotected. Overuse and abuse of your references will lead to less-than-supportive comments. Protect your references by giving out their names only when you are being considered seriously as a candidate for a given position.

## THE FUNCTIONAL RESUME

The functional resume departs from a chronological resume in that it organizes information by specific accomplishments in various settings: previous jobs, volunteer work, associations, etc. This type of resume permits you to stress the substance of your experiences rather than the position titles you have held. (See Exhibit 2.3.) You should consider using a functional resume if you have held a series of similar jobs that relied on the same skills or abilities.

---

**Exhibit 2.3**

### Functional Resume

**JAMES ALLEN HODGES**
345 Fayette Street, Apt. 3
San Francisco, CA 94111
(415) 555-3580

*OBJECTIVE*
A position as a radio announcer in music or news programming that allows me to show my creativity and initiative.

continued

---

continued

## CAPABILITIES
- Excellent communicator
- Strong people skills
- Extensive knowledge of popular music culture

## SELECTED ACCOMPLISHMENTS

ANNOUNCING: Through a college internship, I rotated through several different departments at radio station KGO. My duties included selecting and introducing recorded music; presenting news, sports, weather, and commercials; interviewing guests; reporting on community activities.

TECHNICAL: Operated the control board at KGO and at WBCN in Boston.

TEAM PLAYER: Collaborated with coworkers and professionals in other departments including the news staff and community affairs.

PROMOTION: Participated in several community activities, including broadcasting live at the annual art festival and at the opening of a new music store in San Francisco.

## AWARDS
Dean's List (four semesters)

## PORTFOLIO
Selection of audition tapes and recorded programs available upon request.

## EMPLOYMENT HISTORY
KGO Radio, American Broadcasting Company, San Francisco, CA 1996 to Present
WBCN, Boston, MA Summers 1993 to 1995

## EDUCATION
Bachelor of Arts in Radio Broadcasting
Minor: Music History
University of San Francisco, San Francisco, CA
June 1997

## REFERENCES
Provided upon request.

## The Objective

A functional resume begins with an objective that can be used to focus the contents of the resume.

## Specific Accomplishments

Specific accomplishments are listed on this type of resume. Examples of the types of headings used to describe these capabilities might include sales, counseling, teaching, communication, production, management, marketing, or writing. The headings you choose will directly relate to your experience and the tasks that you carried out. Each accomplishment section contains statements related to your experience in that category, regardless of when or where it occurred. Organize the accomplishments and the related tasks you describe in their order of importance as related to the position you seek.

## Experience or Employment History

Your actual work experience is condensed and placed after the specific accomplishments section. It simply lists dates of employment, position titles, and employer names.

## Education

The education section of a functional resume is identical to that of the chronological resume, but it does not carry the same visual importance because it is placed near the bottom of the page.

## References

Because actual reference names are never listed on a resume, this section is optional if space does not permit.

# THE TARGETED RESUME

The targeted resume focuses on specific work-related capabilities you can bring to a given position within an organization. (See Exhibit 2.4.) It should be sent to an individual within the organization who makes hiring decisions about the position you are seeking.

## The Objective

The objective on this type of resume should be targeted to a specific career or position. It should be supported by the capabilities, accomplishments, and achievements documented in the resume.

**Exhibit 2.4**

## Targeted Resume

### REBECCA SMITH

Gibson Hall, Room 225
University of Denver
Denver, CO 80201
(303) 555-0688
(Until May 1997)

25 West Diplomat Drive
Boulder, CO 83576
(303) 555-6752

*JOB TARGET*
A position as a music librarian with a museum or public or private library.

*CAPABILITIES*
- Developing music education programs
- Coordinating efforts with local schools
- Research skills
- Organizing related events with speakers and presentations
- Familiar with a variety of computer software
- Familiar with computer information systems
- Strong people skills

*ACHIEVEMENTS*
- Codeveloped "Music in Public Places" Program
- Researched information for the Rock-and-Roll Hall of Fame
- Placed several articles in local newspapers
- Graduated with honors

*WORK HISTORY*

1996–1997    Student Internship
Rock-and-Roll Hall of Fame
Cleveland, Ohio
- Nine-month position researching and organizing biographical information on musicians to be inducted

1994–1996    Work Study Position
Assistant Reference Librarian
University of Denver, Main Library
- Assisted students and faculty in locating a variety of reference materials

1993–1994    Summer Position (two summers)
Tour Guide, Hampton House
Boulder, Colorado
- Led tours of historic home, provided visitors with information

continued

continued

***EDUCATION***
1997
Bachelor of Arts in Music with a minor in Library Science
University of Denver, Denver, Colorado

## Capabilities

Capabilities should be statements that illustrate tasks you believe you are capable of based on your accomplishments, achievements, and work history. Each should relate to your targeted career or position. You can stress your qualifications rather than your employment history. This approach may require research to obtain an understanding of the nature of the work involved and the capabilities necessary to carry out that work.

## Accomplishments/Achievements

This section relates the various activities you have been involved in to the job market. These experiences may include previous jobs, extracurricular activities at school, internships, and part-time summer work.

## Experience

Your work history should be listed in abbreviated form and may include position title, employer name, and employment dates.

## Education

Because this type of resume is directed toward a specific job target and an individual's related experience, the education section is not prominently located at the top of the resume as is done on the chronological resume.

# THE BROADCAST LETTER

The broadcast letter is used by some job seekers in place of a resume and cover letter. (See Exhibit 2.5.) The purpose of this type of document is to make a number of potential employers aware of the availability and expertise of the job seeker. Because the broadcast letter is mass-mailed (500–600 employers), the amount of work required may not be worth the return for many people. If you choose to mail out a broadcast letter, you can expect to receive a response from 2–5 percent, at best, of the organizations that receive your letter.

This type of document is most often used by individuals who have an extensive and quantifiable work history. College students often do not have the

**Exhibit 2.5**

## Broadcast Letter

**JACKIE LEE TAYLOR**
5543 Juniper Lane
Houston, Texas 77504
(713) 555-3674

June 6, 1997

Dr. Alden Campbell, Director
Houston Center for Children and Families
3265 Bay Front Road
Houston, TX 77525

Dear Dr. Campbell,

I am writing to you because your center may be in need of a music therapist with a specialization in child development. With my master's degree from UT, Austin, and my four years of progressively increasing experience in a variety of settings, I have had the opportunity to work with a cross section of clients with a range of needs. I am able to adapt to different environments and put my skills and abilities to immediate use. Some highlights of my experience that might interest you include:

- Developed music therapy program for students with learning disabilities in the Austin, Texas, school district. I implemented this program for three years, evaluating student progress and writing reports for funding documentation.

- Supervised bachelor's level occupational therapy majors in work–study positions in the school district.

- Directed the Houston Youth Club Choir, scheduling rehearsals and performances.

I received my BA in 1993 in music and my MA in 1995 in elementary education, both from the University of Texas, Austin.

continued

continued

It would be a pleasure to review my qualifications with you in a personal interview at some mutually convenient time. I will call your office at the end of next week to make arrangements. I look forward to discussing career opportunities with the Houston Center for Children and Families.

Sincerely,


Jackie Lee Taylor

credentials and work experience to support using a broadcast letter, and most will find it difficult to effectively quantify a slim work history.

A broadcast letter is generally five paragraphs (one page) long. The first paragraph should immediately gain the attention of the reader and state some unusual accomplishment or skill that would be of benefit to the organization. The second paragraph states the reason for the letter. Details of the sender's work history are revealed in the third paragraph. Education and other qualifications or credentials are then described. Finally, the job seeker indicates what he or she will do to follow up on the letter, which usually is a follow-up call 1–2 weeks after the letter is sent.

## RESUME PRODUCTION AND OTHER TIPS

If you have the option and convenience of using a laser printer, you may want to initially produce a limited number of copies in case you want or need to make changes on your resume.

Resume paper color should be carefully chosen. You should consider the types of employers who will receive your resume and the types of positions for which you are applying. Use white or ivory paper for traditional or conservative employers, or for higher-level positions.

Black ink on sharply white paper can be harsh on the reader's eyes. Think about an ivory or cream paper that will provide less contrast and be easier to read. Pink, green, and blue tints should generally be avoided.

Many resume writers buy packages of matching envelopes and cover sheet stationery that, although not absolutely necessary, do convey a professional impression.

If you'll be producing many cover letters at home, be sure you have high-quality printing equipment, whether it be computerized or standard typewriter equipment. Learn standard envelope formats for business and retain a copy of every cover letter you send out. You can use it to take notes of any telephone conversations that may occur.

If attending a job fair, women generally can fold their resume in thirds lengthwise and find it fits into a clutch bag or envelope-style purse. Both men and women will have no trouble if they carry a briefcase. For men without a briefcase, carry the resume in a nicely covered legal-size pad holder or fold it in half lengthwise and place it inside your suitcoat pocket, taking care it doesn't "float" outside your collar.

# THE COVER LETTER

The cover letter provides you with the opportunity to tailor your resume by telling the prospective employer how you can be a benefit to the organization. It will allow you to highlight aspects of your background that are not already discussed in your resume and that might be especially relevant to the organization you are contacting or to the position you are seeking. Every resume should have a cover letter enclosed when you send it out. Unlike the resume, which may be mass-produced, a cover letter is most effective when it is individually typed and focused on the particular requirements of the organization in question.

A good cover letter should supplement the resume and motivate the reader to review the resume. The format shown in Exhibit 2.6 is only a suggestion to help you decide what information to include in writing a cover letter.

Begin the cover letter with your street address 12 lines down from the top. Leave three to five lines between the date and the name of the person to whom

---

**Exhibit 2.6**

## Cover Letter Format

Your Street Address
Your Town, State, Zip
Phone Number
Date

continued

continued

Name
Title
Organization
Address


Dear _____:

First Paragraph. In this paragraph, state the reason for the letter, name the specific position or type of work you are applying for, and indicate from which resource (career development office, newspaper, contact, employment service) you learned of the opening. The first paragraph can also be used to inquire about future openings.

Second Paragraph. Indicate why you are interested in the position, the company, its products or services, and what you can do for the employer. If you are a recent graduate, explain how your academic background makes you a qualified candidate. Try not to repeat the same information found in the resume.

Third Paragraph. Refer the reader to the enclosed resume for more detailed information.

Fourth Paragraph. In this paragraph, say what you will do to follow up on your letter. For example, state that you will call by a certain date to set up an interview or to find out if the company will be recruiting in your area. Finish by indicating your willingness to answer any questions they may have. Be sure you have provided your phone number.

Sincerely,



Type your name

Enclosure

you are addressing the cover letter. Make sure you leave one blank line between the salutation and the body of the letter and between each paragraph.

After typing "Sincerely," leave four blank lines and type your name. This should leave plenty of room for your signature. A sample cover letter is shown in Exhibit 2.7.

The following are guidelines that will help you write good cover letters:

1. Be sure to type your letter; ensure there are no misspellings.

---

**Exhibit 2.7**

## Sample Cover Letter

---

JENNIFER RAPHAELI
37 Morning Glory Drive
Ithaca, New York 14807
(607) 555-2126

May 10, 1997

Deborah Hartly
Director of Personnel
Cayuga County School Board
65 Cayuga Street
Ithaca, NY 14807

Dear Ms. Hartly:

In June of 1997 I will graduate from Ithaca College with a Bachelor of Arts degree in Music Education. I read of your opening for a dual secondary-level music teacher and band leader in *The Chronicle of Higher Education* on Wednesday, May 9, 1997, and I am very interested in the possibilities it offers. I am writing to explore the opportunity for employment with your school district.

The ad indicated you were looking for a creative individual with good communication skills and the ability to lead others. I believe I possess those qualities. Through my placement at the Ithaca Day School during my student teaching period I learned the importance of teamwork and encouraging students to express their talents.

In addition to the various music and education courses in my academic program, I felt it important to enroll in some art, psychology, and computer courses such as art history and computer-assisted design (CAD).

These courses helped me become familiar with the wide range of creative influences, while at the same time familiarizing myself with a variety of innovative programs working with children. I believe that this exposure, coupled with my enthusiasm for working in an educational environment, will

continued

continued

help me to represent the Cayuga School Board in a professional and competent manner.

As you will see by my enclosed resume, I worked at the Ithaca Day School and also at several summer camps, where I led the camp choir and helped organize other musical presentations. These placements provided me with experience channeling the creative energies of young children through music expression.

I would like to meet with you to discuss how my education and experience would be consistent with your needs. I will contact your office next week to discuss the possibility of an interview. In the meantime, if you have any questions or require additional information, please contact me at my home, (607) 555-2126.

Sincerely,

Jennifer Raphaeli
Enclosure

2. Avoid unusual typefaces, such as script.

3. Address the letter to an individual, using the person's name and title. To obtain this information, call the company. If answering a blind newspaper advertisement, address the letter "To Whom It May Concern" or omit the salutation.

4. Be sure your cover letter directly indicates the position you are applying for and tells why you are qualified to fill it.

5. Send the original letter, not a photocopy, with your resume. Keep a copy for your records.

6. Make your cover letter no more than one page.

7. Include a phone number where you can be reached.

8. Avoid trite language and have someone read it over to react to its tone, content, and mechanics.

9. For your own information, record the date you send out each letter and resume.

# CHAPTER THREE

# RESEARCHING CAREERS

..................................................

One common question a career counselor encounters is "What can I do with my degree?" Music majors have narrowed their interests a little more successfully than other liberal arts graduates, but still, all the choices are not clearly defined. Music graduates can often struggle with this problem because unlike their fellow students in more applied fields, such as accounting, computer science, or health and physical education, there is real confusion about just what kinds of jobs, other than the obvious route of teaching or performing, they can do with their degree. Accounting majors become accountants, computer science majors can work as data analysts. What jobs are open to music majors?

..................................................

## WHAT DO THEY CALL THE JOB YOU WANT?

There is every reason to be unaware. One reason for confusion is perhaps a mistaken assumption that a college education provides job training. In most cases, it does not. Of course, applied fields such as engineering, management, or education provide specific skills for the workplace, whereas most liberal arts degrees simply provide an education. A liberal arts education exposes you to numerous fields of study and teaches you quantitative reasoning, critical thinking, writing, and speaking, all of which can be successfully applied to a number of different job fields. But it still remains up to you to choose a job field and to learn how to articulate the benefits of your education in a way the employer will appreciate.

As indicated in Chapter 1 on self-assessment, your first task is to understand and value what parts of that education you enjoyed and were good at and would continue to enjoy in your life's work. Did your writing courses encourage you in your ability to express yourself in writing? Did you enjoy the research process and did you find your work was well received? Did you enjoy any of your required quantitative subjects like algebra or calculus?

The answers to questions such as these provide clues to skills and interests you bring to the employment market over and above the credential of your degree. In fact, it is not an overstatement to suggest that most employers who demand a college degree immediately look beyond that degree to you as a person and your own individual expression of what you like to do and think you can do for them, regardless of your major.

## Collecting Job Titles

The world of employment is a big place, and even seasoned veterans of the job hunt can be surprised about what jobs are to be found in what organizations. You need to become a bit of an explorer and adventurer and be willing to try a variety of techniques to begin a list of possible occupations that might use your talents and education. Once you have a list of possibilities that you are interested in and qualified for, you can move on to find out what kinds of organizations have these job titles.

...............................................................

Not every employer seeking to hire a music major may be equally desirable to you. Some employment environments may be more attractive to you than others. A musician wanting to perform could do that with a large orchestra, in a small nightclub, possibly on television or in film, or even at family events such as weddings and bar mitzvahs. Each of these environments presents a different "culture" with associated norms in the pace of work, the subject matter of interest, and the backgrounds of its employees. Although the job titles may be the same, not all locations may present the same "fit" for you.

If you majored in music, enjoyed any in-class presentations you might have done as part of your degree, and have developed a strong stage presence, you might naturally think of performing. But music majors with these same skills and interests can also go on to teach skills to others, or work as music therapists, or become conductors, leading choirs, orchestras, or bands. Each of these job titles can also be found in a number of different settings.

......................................................

Take training, for example. Trainers write policy and procedural manuals and actively teach to assist all levels of employees in mastering various tasks and work-related systems. Trainers exist in all large corporations, banks, consumer goods manufacturers, medical diagnostic equipment firms, sales organizations, and any organization that has processes or materials that need to be presented to and learned by the staff.

In reading job descriptions or want ads for any of these positions, you would find your four-year degree a "must." However, the academic major might be less important than your own individual skills in critical thinking, analysis, report writing, public presentations, and interpersonal communication. Even more important than thinking or knowing you have certain skills is your ability to express those skills concretely and the examples you use to illustrate them to an employer.

The best beginning to a job search is to create a list of job titles you might want to pursue, learn more about the nature of the jobs behind those titles, and then discover what kinds of employers hire for those positions. In the following section, we'll teach you how to build a job title directory to use in your job search.

## Developing a Job Title Directory That Works for You

A job title directory is simply a complete list of all the job titles you are interested in, are intrigued by, or think you are qualified for. Combining the understanding gained through self-assessment with your own individual interests and the skills and talents you've acquired with your degree, you'll soon start to read and recognize a number of occupational titles that seem right for you. There are several resources you can use to develop your list, including computer searches, books, and want ads.

**Computerized Interest Inventories.**   One way to begin your search is to identify a number of jobs that call for your degree and the particular skills and interests you identified as part of the self-assessment process. There are on the market excellent interactive computer career guidance programs to help you produce such selected lists of possible job titles. Most of these are available at high schools and colleges and at some larger town and city libraries. Two of the industry leaders are SIGI and DISCOVER. Both allow you to enter interests, values, educational background, and other information to produce lists of possible occupations and industries. Each of the resources listed here will produce different job title lists. Some job titles will appear again and again, while others will be unique to a particular source. Investigate them all!

**Reference Books.**   Books on the market that may be available through your local library, bookstore, or career counseling office also suggest various occupations related to a number of majors. The following are only two of the many good books on the market: *Occupational Outlook Handbook (OOH)* and *Occupational Projections and Training Data,* both put out by the U.S. Department of Labor, Bureau of Labor Statistics. The *OOH* describes hundreds of job titles under several broad categories such as Executive, Administrative, and Managerial Occupations and also indentifies those jobs by their *Dictionary of Occupational Titles* (DOT) code. (See following discussion.)

·················································

For music majors, more than two dozen related job titles are listed throughout various sections of the *OOH.* Some are familiar ones such as singer or composer. Others are interestingly different, such as choral director, music therapist, or librettist.

The *Occupational Projections and Training Data* is another good resource that essentially allows job seekers to compare five hundred occupations on factors such as job openings, earnings, and training requirements.

So, if as a music major you discover music librarian as a job title in the *OOH,* you can then go to the *Occupational Projections and Training Data* and compare it with scores of jobs related to that title. This source adds some depth by presenting statistics in a number of different occupations within that field.

·················································

Each job title deserves your consideration. Like the layers of an onion, the search for job titles can go on and on! As you spend time doing this activity, you are actually learning more about the value of your degree. What's important in your search at this point is not to become critical or selective, but rather to develop as long a list of possibilities as you can. Every source used will help you add new and potentially exciting jobs to your growing list.

**Want Ads.**   It has been well publicized that newspaper want ads represent only about 10–15 percent of the current job market. Nevertheless, the Sunday want ads can be a great help to you in your search. Although they may not be the best place to look for a job, they can teach the job seeker much about the job market and provide a good education in job descriptions, duties and responsibilities, active industries, and some indication of the volume of job traffic. For our purposes, they are a good source for job titles to add to your list.

Read the Sunday want ads in a major market newspaper for several Sundays in a row. Circle and then cut out any and all ads that interest you and seem to call for something close to your education and experience. Remember, because want ads are written for what an organization *hopes* to find, you don't have to meet absolutely every criterion. However, if certain requirements are stated as absolute minimums and you cannot meet them, it's best not to waste your time.

A recent examination of *The Boston Sunday Globe* reveals the following possible occupations for a liberal arts major with some computer skills and limited prior work experience. (This is only a partial list of what was available.)

- Admissions representative
- Salesperson
- Compliance director
- Assistant principal gifts writer
- Public relations officer
- Technical writer
- Personnel trainee
- GED examiner
- Direct mail researcher
- Associate publicist

After performing this exercise for a few Sundays, you'll find you have collected a new library of job titles.

The Sunday want ad exercise is important because these jobs are out in the marketplace. They truly exist, and people with your qualifications are being sought to apply. What's more, many of these advertisements describe the duties and responsibilities of the job advertised and give you a beginning sense of the challenges and opportunities such a position presents. Some will indicate salary, and that will be helpful as well. This information will better define the jobs for you and provide some good material for possible interviews in that field.

## Exploring Job Descriptions

Once you've arrived at a solid list of possible job titles that interest you and for which you believe you are somewhat qualified, it's a good idea to do some research on each of these jobs. The preeminent source for such job information is the *Dictionary of Occupational Titles,* or DOT. This directory lists every conceivable job and provides excellent up-to-date information on duties and responsibilities, interactions with associates, and day-to-day assignments and tasks. These descriptions provide a thorough job analysis, but they do not consider the possible employers or the environments in which this job may be performed. So, although a position as public relations officer may be well defined in terms of duties and responsibilities, it does not explain the differences in doing public relations work in a college or a hospital or a factory or a bank. You will need to look somewhere else for work settings.

## Learning More about Possible Work Settings

After reading some job descriptions, you may choose to edit and revise your list of job titles once again, discarding those you feel are not suitable and keeping those that continue to hold your interest. Or you may wish to keep your list intact and see where these jobs may be located. For example, if you are interested in public relations and you appear to have those skills and the requisite education, you'll want to know what organizations do public relations. How can you find that out? How much income does someone in public relations make a year and what is the employment potential for the field of public relations?

To answer these and many other good questions about your list of job titles, we will direct you to any of the following resources: *Careers Encyclopedia, Career Information Center, College to Career: The Guide to Job Opportunities,* and the *Occupational Outlook Handbook.* Each of these books, in a different way, will help to put the job titles you have selected into an employer context. *VGM'S Handbook for Business and Management Careers* shows detailed career descriptions for over 50 fields. Entries include complete information on duties and responsibilities for individual careers and detailed entry-level requirements. There is information on working conditions and promotional opportunities as well. Salary ranges and career outlook projections are also provided. Perhaps the most extensive discussion is found in the *Occupational Outlook Handbook,* which gives a thorough presentation of the nature of the work, the working conditions, employment statistics, training, other qualifications, and advancement possibilities as well as job outlook and earnings. Related occupations are also detailed, and a select bibliography is provided to help you find additional information.

Continuing with our public relations example, your search through these reference materials would teach you that the public relations jobs you find attractive are available in larger hospitals, financial institutions, most corporations (both consumer goods and industrial goods), media organizations, and colleges and universities.

## Networking to Get the Complete Story

You now have not only a list of job titles but also, for each of these job titles, a description of the work involved and a general list of possible employment settings in which to work. You'll want to do some reading and keep talking to friends, colleagues, teachers, and others about the possibilities. Don't neglect to ask if the career office at your college maintains some kind of alumni network. Often such alumni networks will connect you with another graduate from the college who is working in the job title or industry you are seeking information about. These career networkers offer what assistance they can. For some, it is a full day "shadowing" the alumnus as he or she goes about the job. Others offer partial day visits, tours, informational interviews, resume reviews, job postings, or, if distance prevents a visit, telephone interviews. As fellow graduates, they'll be frank and informative about their own jobs and prospects in their field.

Take them up on their offer and continue to learn all you can about your own personal list of job titles, descriptions, and employment settings. You'll probably continue to edit and refine this list as you learn more about the realities of the job, the possible salary, advancement opportunities, and supply and demand statistics.

In the next section, we'll describe how to find the specific organizations that represent these industries and employers, so that you can begin to make contact.

## WHERE ARE THESE JOBS, ANYWAY?

Having a list of job titles that you've designed around your own career interests and skills is an excellent beginning. It means you've really thought about who you are and what you are presenting to the employment market. It has caused you to think seriously about the most appealing environments to work in, and you have identified some employer types that represent these environments.

The research and the thinking that you've done this far will be used again and again. It will be helpful in writing your resume and cover letters, in talking about yourself on the telephone to prospective employers, and in answering interview questions.

Now is a good time to begin to narrow the field of job titles and employment sites down to some specific employers to initiate the employment contact.

### Finding Out Which Employers Hire People Like You

This section will provide tips, techniques, and specific resources for developing an actual list of specific employers that can be used to make contacts. It is only an outline that you must be prepared to tailor to your own particular needs and according to what you bring to the job search. Once again, it is important to stress the need to communicate with others along the way exactly what you're looking for and what your goals are for the research you're doing. Librarians, employers, career counselors, friends, friends of friends, business contacts, and bookstore staff will all have helpful information on geographically specific and new resources to aid you in locating employers who'll hire you.

# Identifying Information Resources

Your interview wardrobe and your new resume may have put a dent in your wallet, but the resources you'll need to pursue your job search are available for free (although you might choose to copy materials on a machine instead of taking notes by hand). The categories of information detailed here are not hard to find and are yours for the browsing.

Numerous resources described in this section will help you identify actual employers. Use all of them or any others that you identify as available in your geographic area. As you become experienced in this process, you'll quickly figure out which information sources are helpful and which are not. If you live in a rural area, a well-planned day trip to a major city that includes a college career office, a large college or city library, state and federal employment centers, a chamber of commerce office, and a well-stocked bookstore can produce valuable results.

There are many excellent resources available to help you identify actual job sites. They are categorized into employer directories (usually indexed by product lines and geographic location), geographically based directories (designed to highlight particular cities, regions, or states), career-specific directories (e.g., *Sports Market Place,* which lists tens of thousands of firms involved with sports), periodicals and newspapers, targeted job posting publications, and videos. This is by no means meant to be a complete list of resources, but rather a starting point for identifying useful resources.

Working from the more general references to highly specific resources, we will provide a basic list to help you begin your search. Many of these you'll find easily available. In some cases, reference librarians and others will suggest even better materials for your particular situation. Start to create your own customized bibliography of job search references. Use copying services to save time and to allow you to carry away information about organization mission, location, company officers, phone numbers, and addresses.

**Employer Directories.**   There are many employer directories available to give you the kind of information you need for your job search. Some of our favorites are listed here, but be sure to ask the professionals you are working with to make additional suggestions.

- ❏ *America's Corporate Families* identifies many major U.S. ultimate parent companies and displays corporate family linkage of subsidiaries and divisions. Businesses can be identified by their industrial code.

- ❏ *Million Dollar Directory: America's Leading Public and Private Companies* lists about 160,000 companies.

- ❏ *Moody's* various manuals are intended as guides for investors, so they contain a history of each company. Each manual contains a classification of companies by industries and products.

❑ *Standard and Poor's Register of Corporations* contains listings for 45,000 businesses, some of which are not listed in the *Million Dollar Directory*.

❑ *Job Seeker's Guide to Private and Public Companies* profiles 15,000 employers in four volumes, each covering a different geographic region. Company entries include contact information, business descriptions, and application procedures.

❑ *The Career Guide: Dun's Employment Opportunities Directory* includes more than 5,000 large organizations, including hospitals and local governments. Profiles include an overview and history of the employer as well as opportunities, benefits, and contact names. It contains geographic and industrial indexes and indexes by discipline or internship availability. This guide also includes a state-by-state list of professional personnel consultants and their specialties.

❑ *Professional's Job Finder/Government Job Finder/Non-Profits Job Finder* are specific directories of job services, salary surveys, and periodical listings in which to find advertisements for jobs in the professional, government, or not-for-profit sector.

❑ *Opportunities in Nonprofit Organizations* is a VGM career series edition that opens up the world of not-for-profit by helping you match your interest profile to the aims and objectives of scores of nonprofit employers in business, education, health and medicine, social welfare, science and technology, and many others. There is also a special section on fundraising and development career paths.

❑ *The 100 Best Companies to Sell For* lists companies by industry and provides contact information and describes benefits and corporate culture.

❑ *The 100 Best Companies to Work For in America* rates organizations on several factors including opportunities, job security, and pay.

❑ *Companies That Care* lists organizations that the authors believe are family-friendly. One index organizes information by state.

❑ *Infotrac CD-ROM Business Index* covers business journals and magazines as well as news magazines and can provide information on public and private companies.

❑ *ABI/INFORM On Disc* (CD-ROM) indexes articles in over 800 journals.

**Geographically Based Directories.** The Job Bank series published by Bob Adams, Inc. contains detailed entries on each area's major employers, including business activity, address, phone number, and hiring contact name. Many listings specify educational backgrounds being sought in potential employees. Each volume contains a solid discussion of each city's or state's major employment sectors. Organizations are also indexed by industry. Job Bank volumes are available for the following places: Atlanta, Boston, Chicago, Denver, Dallas–Ft. Worth, Florida, Houston, Ohio, St. Louis, San Francisco, Seattle, Los Angeles, New York, Detroit, Philadelphia, Minneapolis, the Northwest, and Washington, D.C.

*National Job Bank* lists employers in every state, along with contact names and commonly hired job categories. Included are many small companies often overlooked by other directories. Companies are also indexed by industry. This publication provides information on educational backgrounds sought and lists company benefits.

**Career-Specific Directories.**   VGM publishes a number of excellent series detailing careers for college graduates. In the *Professional Career Series* are guides to careers in the following fields, among others:

❑ Advertising

❑ Communications

❑ Business

❑ Computers

❑ Health Care

❑ High Tech

Each provides an excellent discussion of the industry, educational requirements for jobs, salary ranges, duties, and projected outlooks for the field.

Another VGM series, *Opportunities In . . .,* has an equally wide range of titles relating to your major, such as the following:

❑ *Opportunities in Banking*

❑ *Opportunities in Insurance*

❑ *Opportunities in Sports and Athletics*

❑ *Opportunities in Journalism*

❑ *Opportunities in Marketing*

❑ *Opportunities in Television and Radio*

*Sports Market Place* (Sportsguide) lists organizations by sport. It also describes trade/professional associations, college athletic organizations, multi-sport publications, media contacts, corporate sports sponsors, promotion/event/athletic management services, and trade shows.

**Periodicals and Newspapers.**    Several sources are available to help you locate which journals or magazines carry job advertisements in your field. Other resources help you identify opportunities in other parts of the country.

❑ *Where the Jobs Are: A Comprehensive Directory of 1200 Journals Listing Career Opportunities* links specific occupational titles to corresponding periodicals that carry job listings for your field.

❑ *Social & Behavioral Sciences Jobs Handbook* contains a periodicals matrix organized by academic discipline and highlights periodicals containing job listings.

❑ *National Business Employment Weekly* compiles want ads from four regional editions of the *Wall Street Journal.* Most are business and management positions.

❑ *National Ad Search* reprints ads from 75 metropolitan newspapers across the country. Although the focus is on management positions, technical and professional postings are also included. *Caution:* Watch deadline dates carefully on listings, because deadlines may have already passed by the time the ad is printed.

❑ *The Federal Jobs Digest* and *Federal Career Opportunities* list government positions.

❑ *World Chamber of Commerce Directory* lists addresses for chambers worldwide, state boards of tourism, convention and visitors' bureaus, and economic development organizations.

This list is certainly not exhaustive; use it to begin your job search work.

**Targeted Job Posting Publications.**    Although the resources that follow are national in scope, they are either targeted to one medium of contact (telephone), focused on specific types of jobs, or are less comprehensive than the sources previously listed.

❑ *Job Hotlines USA* pinpoints over 1,000 hard-to-find telephone numbers for companies and government agencies that use prerecorded job messages and listings. Very few of the telephone numbers listed are toll-free, and sometimes recordings are long, so callers beware!

❑ *The Job Hunter* is a national biweekly newspaper listing business, arts, media, government, human services, health, community-related, and student services job openings.

❑ *Current Jobs for Graduates* is a national employment listing for liberal arts professions, including editorial positions, management opportunities, museum work, teaching, and nonprofit work.

❑ *Environmental Opportunities* serves environmental job interests nation-wide by listing administrative, marketing, and human resources positions along with education-related jobs and positions directly related to a degree in an environmental field.

❑ *Y National Vacancy List* shows YMCA professional vacancies, including development, administration, programming, membership, and recreation postings.

❑ *ARTSearch* is a national employment service bulletin for the arts, including administration, managerial, marketing, and financial management jobs.

❑ *Community Jobs* is an employment newspaper for the nonprofit sector that provides a variety of listings, including project manager, canvas director, government relations specialist, community organizer, and program instructor.

❑ *College Placement Council Annual: A Guide to Employment Opportunities for College Graduates* is an annual guide containing solid job-hunting information and, more importantly, displaying ads from large corporations actively seeking recent college graduates in all majors. Company profiles provide brief descriptions and available employment opportunities. Contact names and addresses are given. Profiles are indexed by organization name, geographic location, and occupation.

**Videos.** You may be one of the many job seekers who like to get information via a medium other than paper. Many career libraries, public libraries, and career centers in libraries carry an assortment of videos that will help you learn new techniques and get information helpful in the job search. A small sampling of the multitude of videos now available includes the following:

❑ *The Skills Search* (20 min.) discusses three types of skills important in the workplace, how to present the skills in an interview, and how to respond to problem questions.

❑ *Effective Answers to Interview Questions* (35 min.) presents two real-life job seekers and shows how they realized the true meaning of interview questions and formulated positive answers.

❑ *Employer's Expectations* (33 min.) covers three areas that are important to all employers: appearance, dependability, and skills.

❑ *The Tough New Labor Market of the 1990s* (30 min.) presents labor market facts as well as suggestions on what job seekers should do to gain employment in this market.

❑ *Dialing for Jobs: Using the Phone in the Job Search* (30 min.) describes how to use the phone effectively to gain information and arrange interviews by following two new graduates as they learn and apply techniques.

## Locating Information Resources

An essay by John Case that appeared in the *Boston Globe* (August 25, 1993) alerts both new and seasoned job seekers that the job market is changing, and the old guarantees of lifelong employment no longer hold true. Some of our major corporations, which were once seen as the most prestigious of employment destinations, are now laying off thousands of employees. Middle management is especially hard hit in downsizing situations. On the other side of the coin, smaller, more entrepreneurial firms are adding employees and realizing enormous profit margins. The geography of the new job market is unfamiliar, and the terrain is much harder to map. New and smaller firms can mean different kinds of jobs and new job titles. The successful job seeker will keep an open mind about where he or she might find employment and what that employment might be called.

In order to become familiar with this new terrain, you will need to undertake some research, which can be done at any of the following locations:

❑ Public libraries

❑ Business organizations

❑ Employment agencies

❑ Bookstores

❑ Career libraries

Each one of these places offers a collection of resources that will help you get the information you need.

As you meet and talk with service professionals at all these sites, be sure to let them know what you're doing. Inform them of your job search, what you've already accomplished, and what you're looking for. The more people who know you're job seeking, the greater the possibility that someone will have information or know someone who can help you along your way.

**Public Libraries.**   Large city libraries, college and university libraries, and even well-supported town library collections contain a variety of resources to help you conduct a job search. It is not uncommon for libraries to have separate "vocational choices" sections with books, tapes, and associated materials relating to job search and selection. Some are now even making resume creation software available for use by patrons.

Some of the publications we name throughout this book are expensive reference items that are rarely purchased by individuals. In addition, libraries carry a wide range of newspapers and telephone yellow pages as well as the usual array of books. If resources are not immediately available, many libraries have loan arrangements with other facilities and can make information available to you relatively quickly.

Take advantage of not only the reference collections, but also the skilled and informed staff. Let them know exactly what you are looking for, and they'll have their own suggestions. You'll be visiting the library frequently, and the reference staff will soon come to know who you are and what you're working on. They'll be part of your job search network!

**Business Organizations.**   Chambers of Commerce, Offices of New Business Development, Councils on Business and Industry, Small Business Administration (SBA) offices, and professional associations can all provide geographically specific lists of companies and organizations that have hiring needs. They also have an array of other available materials, including visitors' guides and regional fact books that provide additional employment information.

These agencies serve to promote local and regional businesses and ensure their survival and success. Although these business organizations do not advertise job openings or seek employees for their members, they may be very aware of staffing needs among their member firms. In your visits to each of these locations, spend some time with the personnel getting to know who they are and what they do. Let them know of your job search and your intentions regarding employment. You may be surprised and delighted at the information they may provide.

**Employment Agencies.**   Employment agencies, including state and federal employment offices, professional "head hunters" or executive search firms, and some private career counselors can provide direct leads to job openings. Don't overlook these resources. If you are mounting a complete job search program and want to ensure that you are covering the potential market for employers, consider the employment agencies in your territory. Some of these organizations work contractually with several specific firms and may have access that is unavailable to you. Others may be particularly well informed about supply and demand in particular industries or geographic locations.

In the case of professional (commercial) employment agencies, which include those executive recruitment firms labeled "head hunters," you should be cautious about entering into any binding contractual agreement. Before doing so, be sure to get the information you need to decide whether their services can be of use to you. Questions to ask include the following: Who pays the fee when employment is obtained? Are there any other fees or costs associated with this service? What is their placement rate? Can you see a list of previous clients and can you talk to any for references? Do they typically work with entry-level job seekers? Do they tend to focus on particular kinds of employment or industries?

A few cautions are in order, however, when you work with professional agencies. Remember, the professional employment agency is, in most cases, paid by the hiring organization. Naturally, their interest and attention is largely directed to the employer, not to the candidate. Of course, they want to provide good candidates to guarantee future contracts, but they are less interested in the job seeker than the employer.

For teacher candidates, there are a number of good placement firms that charge the prospective teacher, not the employer. This situation has evolved over time as a result of supply and demand and financial structuring of most school systems, which cannot spend money on recruiting teachers. Usually these firms charge a nonrefundable administrative fee and, upon successful placement, require a fee based on percentage of salary, which may range from 10–20 percent of annual compensation. Often, this can be repaid over a number of months. Check your contract carefully.

State and federal employment offices are no-fee services that maintain extensive "job boards" and can provide detailed specifications for each job advertised and help with application forms. Because government employment application forms are detailed, keep a master copy along with copies of all additional documentation (resumes, educational transcripts, military discharge papers, proof of citizenship, etc.). Successive applications may require separate filings. Visit these offices as frequently as you can, because most deal with applicants on a "walk-in" basis and will not telephone prospective candidates or maintain files of job seekers. Check your telephone book for the address of the nearest state and federal offices.

One type of employment service that causes much confusion among job seekers is the outplacement firm. Their advertisements tend to suggest they will put you in touch with the "hidden job market." They use advertising phrases such as "We'll work with you until you get that job," or "Maximize your earnings and career opportunities." In fact, if you read the fine print on these ads, you will notice these firms must state they are "Not an employment agency." These firms are, in fact, corporate and private outplacement counseling agencies whose work involves resume editing, counseling to provide leads for jobs, interview skills training, and all the other aspects of hiring preparation. They do this for a fee, sometimes in the thousands of dollars, which is paid by you, the client. Some of these firms have good reputations and provide excellent materials and techniques. Most, however, provide a service you as a college student or graduate can receive free from your alma mater or through a reciprocity agreement between your college and a college or university located closer to your current address.

**Bookstores.**   Any well-stocked bookstore will carry some job search books that are worth buying. Some major stores will even have an extensive section devoted to materials, including excellent videos, related to the job search process. Several possibilities are listed in following sections. You will also find copies of local newspapers and business magazines. The one advantage that is provided by resources purchased at a bookstore is that you can read and work with the information in the comfort of your own home and do not have to conform to the hours of operation of a library, which can present real difficulties if you are working full time as you seek employment. A few minutes spent browsing in a bookstore might be a beneficial break from your job search activities and turn up valuable resources.

**Career Libraries.**   Career libraries, which are found in career centers at colleges and universities and sometimes within large public libraries, contain a unique blend of the job search resources housed in other settings. In addition, career libraries often purchase a number of job listing publications, each of which targets a specific industry or type of job. You may find job listings specifically for entry-level positions for liberal arts majors. Ask about job posting newsletters or newspapers specifically focused on careers in the area that most interests you. Each center will be unique, but you are certain to discover some good sources of jobs.

Most college career libraries now hold growing collections of video material on specific industries and on aspects of your job search process, including dress and appearance, how to manage the luncheon or dinner interview, how to be effective at a job fair, and many other specific titles. Some larger corporations produce handsome video materials detailing the variety of career paths and opportunities available in their organizations.

Some career libraries also house computer-based career planning and information systems. These interactive computer programs help you to clarify your values and interests and will combine that with your education to provide possible job titles and industry locations. Some even contain extensive lists of graduate school programs.

One specific kind of service a career library will be able to direct you to is computerized job search services. These services, of which there are many, are run by private companies, individual colleges, or consortiums of colleges. They attempt to match qualified job candidates with potential employers. The candidate submits a resume (or an application) to the service. This information (which can be categorized into hundreds of separate "fields" of data) is entered into a computer database. Your information is then compared with the information from employers about what they desire in a prospective employee. If there is a "match" between what they want and what you have indicated you can offer, the job search service or the employer will contact you directly to continue the process.

Computerized job search services can complement an otherwise complete job search program. They are *not,* however, a substitute for the kinds of activities described in this book. They are essentially passive operations that are random in nature. If you have not listed skills, abilities, traits, experiences, or education *exactly* as an employer has listed its needs, there is simply no match.

Consult with the staff members at the career libraries you use. These professionals have been specifically trained to meet the unique needs you present. Often you can just drop in and receive help with general questions, or you may want to set up an appointment to speak one-on-one with a career counselor to gain special assistance.

Every career library is different in size and content, but each can provide valuable information for the job search. Some may even provide some limited counseling. If you have not visited the career library at your college or alma mater, call and ask if these collections are still available for your use. Be sure to ask about other services that you can use as well.

If you are not near your own college as you work on your job search, call the career office and inquire about reciprocal agreements with other colleges that are closer to where you live. Very often, your own alma mater can arrange for you to use a limited menu of services at another school. This typically would include access to a career library and job posting information and might include limited counseling.

# CHAPTER fOUR

# NETWORKING

*N*etworking is the process of deliberately establishing relationships to get career-related information or to alert potential employers that you are available for work. Networking is critically important to today's job seeker for two reasons: it will help you get the information you need, and it can help you find out about *all* of the available jobs.

## Getting the Information You Need

Networkers will review your resume and give you candid feedback on its effectiveness. They will talk about the job you are looking for and give you a candid appraisal of how they see your strengths and weaknesses. If they have a good sense of the industry or the employment sector for that job, you'll get their feelings on future trends in the industry as well. Some networkers will be very candid about salaries, job hunting techniques, and suggestions for your job search strategy. Many have been known to place calls right from the interview desk to friends and associates that might be interested in you. Each networker will make his or her own contribution, and each will be valuable.

Because organizations must evolve to adapt to current global market needs, the information provided by decision makers within various organizations will be critical to your success as a new job market entrant. For example, you might learn about the concept of virtual organizations from a networker. Virtual organizations are those that are temporarily established to take advantage of fast-changing opportunities and then dissolved. This concept is being discussed and implemented by chief executive officers of many organizations, including Corning, Apple, and Digital. Networking can help you find out about this and other trends currently affecting the industries under your consideration.

## Finding Out about All of the Available Jobs

Secondly, not every job that is available at this very moment is advertised for potential applicants to see. This is called the *hidden job market*. Only 15–20 percent of all jobs are formally advertised, which means that 80–85 percent of available jobs do not appear in published channels. Networking will help you become more knowledgeable about all the employment opportunities available during your job search period.

Although someone you might talk to today doesn't know of any openings within his or her organization, tomorrow or next week or next month an opening may occur. If you've taken the time to show an interest in and knowledge of their organization, if you've shown the company representative how you can help achieve organizational goals and that you can fit into the organization, you'll be one of the first candidates considered for the position.

## Networking: A Proactive Approach

Networking is a proactive rather than a reactive approach. You, as a job seeker, are expected to initiate a certain level of activity on your own behalf; you cannot afford to simply respond to jobs listed in the newspaper. Being proactive means building a network of contacts that includes informed and interested decision makers who will provide you with up-to-date knowledge of the current job market and increase your chances of finding out about employment opportunities appropriate for your interests, experience, and level of education.

An old axiom of networking says, "You are only two phone calls away from the information you need." In other words, by talking to enough people, you will quickly come across someone who can offer you help. Start with your professors. Each of them probably has a wide circle of contacts. In their work and travel they might have met someone who can help you or direct you to someone who can.

## Control and the Networking Process

In deliberately establishing relationships, the process of networking begins with you in control—*you* are contacting specific individuals. As your network expands and you establish a set of professional relationships, your search for information or jobs will begin to move outside of your total control. A part of the networking process involves others assisting you by gathering information for you or recommending you as a possible job candidate. As additional people become a part of your networking system, you will have less knowledge about activities undertaken on your behalf; you will undoubtedly be contacted by individuals whom you did not initially approach. If you want to function effectively in surprise situations, you must be prepared at all times to talk with strangers about the informational or employment needs that motivated you to become involved in the networking process.

# PREPARING TO NETWORK

In deliberately establishing relationships, maximize your efforts by organizing your approach. Five specific areas in which you can organize your efforts include reviewing your self-assessment, reviewing your research on job sites and organizations, deciding who it is you want to talk to, keeping track of all your efforts, and creating your self-promotion tools.

## Review Your Self-Assessment

Your self-assessment is as important a tool in preparing to network as it has been in other aspects of your job search. You have carefully evaluated your personal traits, personal values, economic needs, longer-term goals, skill base, preferred skills, and underdeveloped skills. During the networking process you will be called upon to communicate what you know about yourself and relate it to the information or job you seek. Be sure to review the exercises that you completed in the self-assessment section of this book in preparation for networking. We've explained that you need to assess what skills you have acquired from your major that are of general value to an employer and to be ready to express those in ways employers can appreciate as useful in their own organizations.

## Review Researching Job Sites and Organizations

In addition, individuals assisting you will expect that you'll have at least some background information on the occupation or industry of interest to you. Refer to the appropriate sections of this book and other relevant publications to acquire the background information necessary for effective networking. They'll explain how to identify not only the job titles that might be of interest to you, but also what kinds of organizations employ people to do that job. You will develop some sense of working conditions and expectations about duties and responsibilities—all of which will be of help in your networking interviews.

## Decide Who It Is You Want to Talk To

Networking cannot begin until you decide who it is that you want to talk to and, in general, what type of information you hope to gain from your contacts. Once you know this, it's time to begin developing a list of contacts. Five useful sources for locating contacts are described here.

**College Alumni Network.**   Most colleges and universities have created a formal network of alumni and friends of the institution who are particularly interested in helping currently enrolled students and graduates of their alma mater gain employment-related information.

..............................................

Because music is such a flexible degree program, you'll find an abundance of music graduates spanning the full spectrum of possible employment. Just the diversity alone evidenced by such an alumni list should be encouraging and informative to the music graduate. Among such a diversified group there are likely to be many you would enjoy talking with and perhaps could meet. Some might be working quite far from you, but that does not preclude a telephone call or exchange of correspondence.

..............................................

It is usually a simple process to make use of an alumni network. You need only visit the alumni or career office at your college or university and follow the procedure that has been established. Often, you will simply complete a form indicating your career goals and interests and you will be given the names of appropriate individuals to contact. In many cases, staff members will coach you on how to make the best use of the limited time these alumni contacts may have available for you.

Alumni networkers may provide some combination of the following services: day-long shadowing experiences, telephone interviews, in-person interviews, information on relocating to given geographic areas, internship information, suggestions on graduate school study, and job vacancy notices.

..............................................

What a valuable experience! Perhaps you are interested in working as a recording musician but you are concerned about your preparation and whether you have a chance, based on the competition in the industry. Spending a day with an alumnus who is a working musician, asking lots of questions about training and preparation, will give you a more concrete view of the possibilities for your career. Learning firsthand how this person got started and observing how he or she does the job will be a far better decision criterion for you than any reading on the subject could possibly provide.

In addition to your own observations, the alumnus will have his or her own perspective on the relevance of your training and will give you realistic and honest feedback on your chances in this area.

..............................................

**Present and Former Supervisors.** If you believe you are on good terms with present or former job supervisors, they may be an excellent resource for providing information or directing you to appropriate resources that would have information related to your current interests and needs. Additionally, these supervisors probably belong to professional organizations, which they might be willing to utilize to get information for you.

..................................................

**If, for example, you were interested in working for a major music store chain and you are currently working on the wait staff of a local restaurant, talk with your supervisor or the owner. He or she may belong to the Chamber of Commerce, whose director would have information on local branches of the chain that are in need of help. You would be able to obtain the names and telephone numbers of these people, thus enabling you to begin the networking process.**

..................................................

**Employers in Your Area.**   Although you may be interested in working in a geographic location different from the one where you currently reside, don't overlook the value of the knowledge and contacts those around you are able to provide. Use the local telephone directory and newspaper to identify the types of organizations you are thinking of working for or professionals who have the kinds of jobs you are interested in. Recently, a call made to a local hospital's financial administrator for information on working in health care financial administration yielded more pertinent information on training seminars, regional professional organizations, and potential employment sites than a national organization was willing to provide.

**Employers in Geographic Areas Where You Hope to Work.**   If you are thinking about relocating, identifying prospective employers or informational contacts in this new location will be critical to your success. Many resources are available to help you locate contact names. These include the yellow pages directory, the local newspapers, local or state business publications, and local Chambers of Commerce.

**Professional Associations and Organizations.**   Professional associations and organizations can provide valuable information in several areas: career paths that you may not have considered, qualifications relating to those career choices, publications that list current job openings, and workshops or seminars that will enhance your professional knowledge and skills. They can also be excellent sources for background information on given industries: their health, current problems, and future challenges.

There are several excellent resources available to help you locate professional associations and organizations that would have information to meet your needs. Two especially useful publications are the *Encyclopedia of Associations* and the *National Trade and Professional Associations of the United States.*

## Keep Track of All Your Efforts

It can be difficult, almost impossible, to remember all the details related to each contact you make during the networking process, so you will want to develop a record-keeping system that works for you. Formalize this process by using a notebook or index cards to organize the information you gather. Begin by creating a list of the people or organizations you want to contact. Record the contact's name, address, telephone number, and what information you hope to gain. Each entry might look something like this:

| Contact Name | Address | Phone # | Purpose |
|---|---|---|---|
| Mr. Tim Keefe | Wrigley Bldg. | | |
| Dir. of Mines | Suite 72 | 555-8906 | Resume screen |

Once you have created this initial list, it will be helpful to keep more detailed information as you begin to actually make the contacts. Using the Network Contact Record form in Exhibit 4.1, keep good information on all your network contacts. They'll appreciate your recall of details of your meetings and conversations, and the information will help you to focus your networking efforts.

---

**Exhibit 4.1**

## Network Contact Record

**Name:** Be certain your spelling is absolutely correct.

**Title:** Pick up a business card to be certain of the correct title.

**Employing organization:** Note any parent company or subsidiaries.

**Business mailing address:** This is often different from the street address.

**Business telephone number:** Include area code/alternative numbers/fax.

**Source for this contact:** Who referred you, and what is their relationship?

continued

continued

**Date of call or letter:** Use plenty of space here to record multiple phone calls or visits, other employees you may have met, names of secretaries/ receptionists, etc.

**Content of discussion:** Keep enough notes here to remind you of the substance of your visits and telephone conversations in case some time elapses between contacts.

**Follow-up necessary to continue working with this contact:**
Your contact may request that you send them some materials or direct you to contact an associate. Note any such instructions or assignments in this space.

**Name of additional networker:** Here you would record the names
**Address:** and phone numbers of additional
**Phone:** contacts met at this employer's
**Name of additional networker:** site. Often you will be introduced to
**Address:** many people, some of whom may
**Phone:** indicate a willingness to help in
**Name of additional networker:** your job search.
**Address:**
**Phone:**

**Date thank-you note written:** May help to date your next contact.

**Follow-up action taken:** Phone calls, visits, additional notes.

**Other miscellaneous notes:** Record any other additional interaction you may find is important to remember in working with this networking client. You will want this form in front of you when telephoning or just before and after a visit.

## Create Your Self-Promotion Tools

There are two types of promotional tools that are used in the networking process. The first is a resume and cover letter, and the second is a one-minute "infomercial," which may be given over the telephone or in person.

Techniques for writing an effective resume and cover letter are covered in Chapter 2. Once you have reviewed that material and prepared these important documents, you will have created one of your self-promotion tools.

The one-minute infomercial will demand that you begin tying your interests, abilities, and skills to the people or organizations you want to network with. Think about your goal for making the contact to help you understand what you should say about yourself. You should be able to express yourself easily and convincingly. If, for example, you are contacting an alumna of your institution to obtain the names of possible employment sites in a distant city, be prepared to discuss why you are interested in moving to that location, the types of jobs you are interested in, and the skills and abilities you possess that will make you a qualified candidate.

To create a meaningful one-minute infomercial, write it out, practice it if it will be a spoken presentation, rewrite it, and practice it again if necessary until expressing yourself comes easily and is convincing.

Here's a simplified example of an infomercial for use over the telephone:

························································

Hello, Mr. Howard? My name is Janet Black. I am a recent graduate of State College, and I wish to enter the broadcasting field in radio. I was a music major and feel confident I have many of the skills I understand are valued in broadcasting, such as a good radio voice, experience with electronic equipment, and a thorough familiarity with popular music and culture. What's more, I work well under pressure. I have read that can be a real advantage in your business!

Mr. Howard, I'm calling you because I still need more information about the broadcasting field. I'm hoping you'll have time to sit down with me for about half an hour and discuss your perspective on radio careers. There are so many possible areas in broadcasting, and I am seeking some advice on which of those areas might be the best bet for my particular combination of skills and experience.

Would you be willing to do that for me? I would greatly appreciate it. I am available most mornings, if that's convenient for you.

························································

Other effective self-promotion tools include portfolios for those in the arts, writing professions, or teaching. Portfolios show examples of work, photographs of projects or classroom activities, or certificates and credentials that are job related. There may not be an opportunity to use the portfolio during an interview, and it is not something that should be left with the organization. It is designed to be explained and displayed by the creator. However, during some networking meetings, there may be an opportunity to illustrate a point or strengthen a qualification by exhibiting the portfolio.

## Beginning the Networking Process

### Set the Tone for Your Contacts

It can be useful to establish "tone words" for any communications you embark upon. Before making your first telephone call or writing your first letter, decide what you want your contact to think of you. If you are networking to try to obtain a job, your tone words might include works like *genuine, informed,* and *self-knowledgeable.* When trying to acquire information, your tone words may have a slightly different focus, such as *courteous, organized, focused,* and *well spoken.* Use the tone words you establish for your contacts to guide you through the networking process.

### Honestly Express Your Intentions

When contacting individuals, it is important to be honest about your reasons for making the contact. Establish your purpose in your own mind and be able and ready to articulate it concisely. Determine an initial agenda, whether it be informational questioning or self-promotion, present it to your contact, and be ready to respond immediately. If you don't adequately prepare before initiating your contacts, you may find yourself at a disadvantage if you're asked to immediately begin your informational interview or self-promotion during the first phone conversation or visit.

### Start Networking Within Your Circle of Confidence

Once you have organized your approach—by utilizing specific researching methods, creating a system for keeping track of the people you will contact, and developing effective self-promotion tools—you are ready to begin networking. The best place to begin networking is by talking with a group of people you trust and feel comfortable with. This group is usually made up of your family, friends, and career counselors. No matter who is in this inner circle, they will have a special interest in seeing you succeed in your job search. In addition, because they will be easy to talk to, you should try taking some risks in terms of practicing your information-seeking approach. Gain confidence in talking about the strengths you bring to an organization and the underdeveloped skills you feel hinder your candidacy. Be sure to review the section on self-assessment for tips on approaching each of these areas. Ask for critical but constructive feedback from the people in your circle of confidence on the letters you write and the one-minute infomercial you have developed. Evaluate whether you want to make the changes they suggest, then practice the changes on others within this circle.

## Stretch the Boundaries of Your Networking Circle of Confidence

Once you have refined the promotional tools you will use to accomplish your networking goals, you will want to make additional contacts. Because you will not know most of these people, it will be a less comfortable activity to undertake. The practice that you gained with your inner circle of trusted friends should have prepared you to now move outside of that comfort zone.

It is said that any information a person needs is only two phone calls away, but the information cannot be gained until you (1) make a reasonable guess about who might have the information you need and (2) pick up the telephone to make the call. Using your network list that includes alumni, instructors, supervisors, employers, and associations, you can begin preparing your list of questions that will allow you to get the information you need. Review the question list shown below and then develop a list of your own.

## Questions You Might Want to Ask

1. In the position you now hold, what do you do on a typical day?

2. What are the most interesting aspects of your job?

3. What part of your work do you consider dull or repetitious?

4. What were the jobs you had that led to your present position?

5. How long does it usually take to move from one step to the next in this career path?

6. What is the top position to which you can aspire in this career path?

7. What is the next step in *your* career path?

8. Are there positions in this field that are similar to your position?

9. What are the required qualifications and training for entry-level positions in this field?

10. Are there specific courses a student should take to be qualified to work in this field?

11. What are the entry-level jobs in this field?

12. What types of training are provided to persons entering this field?

13. What are the salary ranges your organization typically offers to entry-level candidates for positions in this field?

14. What special advice would you give a person entering this field?

15. Do you see this field as a growing one?

16. How do you see the content of the entry-level jobs in this field changing over the next two years?

17. What can I do to prepare myself for these changes?

18. What is the best way to obtain a position that will start me on a career in this field?

19. Do you have any information on job specifications and descriptions that I may have?

20. What related occupational fields would you suggest I explore?

21. How could I improve my resume for a career in this field?

22. Who else would you suggest I talk to, both in your organization and in other organizations?

## Questions You Might Have to Answer

In order to communicate effectively, you must anticipate questions that will be asked of you by the networkers you contact. Review the list below and see if you can easily answer each of these questions. If you cannot, it may be time to revisit the self-assessment process.

1. Where did you get my name, or how did you find out about this organization?

2. What are your career goals?

3. What kind of job are you interested in?

4. What do you know about this organization and this industry?

5. How do you know you're prepared to undertake an entry-level position in this industry?

6. What course work have you taken that is related to your career interests?

7. What are your short-term career goals?

8. What are your long-term career goals?

9. Do you plan to obtain additional formal education?

10. What contributions have you made to previous employers?

11. Which of your previous jobs have you enjoyed the most, and why?

12. What are you particularly good at doing?

13. What shortcomings have you had to face in previous employment?

14. What are your three greatest strengths?

15. Describe how comfortable you feel with your communication style.

## General Networking Tips

**Make Every Contact Count.**   Setting the tone for each interaction is critical. Approaches that will help you communicate in an effective way include politeness, being appreciative of time provided to you, and being prepared and thorough. Remember, *everyone* within an organization has a circle of influence, so be prepared to interact effectively with each person you encounter in the networking process, including secretarial and support staff. Many information or job seekers have thwarted their own efforts by being rude to some individuals they encountered as they networked because they made the incorrect assumption that certain persons were unimportant.

Sometimes your contacts may be surprised at their ability to help you. After meeting and talking with you, they might think they have not offered much in the way of help. A day or two later, however, they may make a contact that would be useful to you and refer you to it.

**With Each Contact, Widen Your Circle of Networkers.**   Always leave an informational interview with the names of at least two more people who can help you get the information or job that you are seeking. Don't be shy about asking for additional contacts; networking is all about increasing the number of people you can interact with to achieve your goals.

**Make Your Own Decisions.**   As you talk with different people and get answers to the questions you pose, you may hear conflicting information or get conflicting suggestions. Your job is to listen to these "experts" and decide what information and which suggestions will help you achieve *your* goals. Only implement those suggestions that you believe will work for you.

# SHUTTING DOWN YOUR NETWORK

As you achieve the goals that motivated your networking activity—getting the information you need or the job you want—the time will come to inactivate all or parts of your network. As you do so, be sure to tell your primary supporters about your change in status. Call or write to each one of them and give them as many details about your new status as you feel is necessary to maintain a positive relationship.

Because a network takes on a life of its own, activity undertaken on your behalf will continue even after you cease your efforts. As you get calls or are contacted in some fashion, be sure to inform these networkers about your change in status, and thank them for assistance they have provided.

Information on the latest employment trends indicates that workers will change jobs or careers several times in their lifetime. If you carefully and thoughtfully conduct your networking activities now, you will have solid experience when you need to network again.

# CHAPTER FIVE

# INTERVIEWING

*C*ertainly, there can be no one part of the job search process more fraught with anxiety and worry than the interview. Yet seasoned job seekers welcome the interview and will often say, "Just get me an interview and I'm on my way!" They understand that the interview is crucial to the hiring process and equally crucial for them, as job candidates, to have the opportunity of a personal dialogue to add to what the employer may already have learned from a resume, cover letter, and telephone conversations.

Believe it or not, the interview is to be welcomed, and even enjoyed! It is a perfect opportunity for you, the candidate, to sit down with an employer and express yourself and display who you are and what you want. Of course, it takes thought and planning and a little strategy; after all, it *is* a job interview! But it can be a positive, if not pleasant, experience and one you can look back on and feel confident about your performance and effort.

For many new job seekers, a job, any job, seems a wonderful thing. But seasoned interview veterans know that the job interview is an important step for both sides—the employer and the candidate—to see what each has to offer and whether there is going to be a "fit" of personalities, work styles, and attitudes. And it is this concept of balance in the interview, that both sides have important parts to play, that holds the key to success in mastering this aspect of the job search strategy.

Try to think of the interview as a conversation between two interested and equal partners. You both have important, even vital, information to deliver and to learn. Of course, there's no denying the employer has some leverage, especially in the initial interview for recruitment or any interview scheduled by the candidate and not the recruiter. That should not prevent the interviewee from seeking to play an equal part in what should be a fair exchange of information. Too often the untutored candidate allows the interview to become one-sided. The employer asks all the questions and the candidate simply responds. The ideal would be for two mutually interested parties to sit down and discuss possibilities for each. For this is a *conversation of significance,* and it requires pre-interview preparation, thought about the tone of the interview, and planning of the nature and details of the information to be exchanged.

## PREPARING FOR THE INTERVIEW

Most initial interviews are about 30 minutes long. Given the brevity, the information that is exchanged ought to be important. The candidate should be delivering material that the employer cannot discover on the resume and, in turn, the candidate should be learning things about the employer that he or she could not otherwise find out. After all, if you have only 30 minutes, why waste time on information that is already published? Not all the information exchanged is factual, and both sides will learn much from what they see of each other, as well. How the candidate looks, speaks, and acts is important to the employer. The employer's attention to the interview and awareness of the candidate's resume, the setting, and the quality of information presented are important to the candidate.

Just as the employer has every right to be disappointed when a prospect is late for the interview, looks unkempt, and seems ill prepared to answer fairly standard questions, the candidate may be disappointed with an interviewer who isn't ready for the meeting, hasn't learned the basic resume facts, and is constantly interrupted for telephone calls. In either situation, there's good reason to feel let down.

There are many elements to a successful interview, and some of them are not easy to describe or prepare for. Sometimes there is just a chemistry between interviewer and interviewee that brings out the best in both, and a good exchange takes place. But there is much the candidate can do to pave the way for success in terms of his or her resume, personal appearance, goals, and interview strategy—each of which we will discuss. However, none of this preparation is as important as the time and thought the candidate gives to personal self-assessment.

### Self-Assessment

Neither a stunning resume nor an expensive, well-tailored suit can compensate for candidates who do not know what they want, where they are going, or why they are interviewing with a particular employer. Self-assessment, the process by which we begin to know and acknowledge our own particular blend of education, experiences, needs, and goals is not something that can be sorted out the weekend before a major interview. Of all the elements of interview preparation, this one requires the longest lead time and cannot be faked.

Because the time allotted for most interviews is brief, it is all the more important for job candidates to understand and express succinctly why they are there and what they have to offer. This is not a time for undue modesty or for braggadocio, either; but it is a time for a compelling, reasoned statement of why you feel that you and this employer might make a good match. It means you have to have thought about your skills, interests, and attributes; related those to your life experiences and your own history of challenges and opportunities; and determined what that indicates about your strengths, preferences, values, and areas needing further development.

A common complaint of employers is that many candidates didn't take advantage of the interview time, didn't seem to know why they were there or what they wanted. When asked to talk about themselves and their work-related skills and attributes, employers don't want to be faced with shyness or embarrassed laughter; they need to know about you so they can make a fair determination of you and your competition. If you lose the opportunity to make a case for your employability, you can be certain the person ahead of you has or the person after you will, and it will be on the strength of those impressions that the employer will hire.

If you need some assistance with self-assessment issues, refer to Chapter 1. Included are suggested exercises that can be done as needed, such as making up an experiential diary and extracting obvious strengths and weaknesses from past experiences. These simple, pen-and-paper assignments will help you look at past activities as collections of tasks with accompanying skills and responsibilities. Don't overlook your high school or college career office, as well. Many offer personal counseling on self-assessment issues and may provide testing instruments such as the Myers-Briggs Type Indicator (MBTI)®, the Harrington-O'Shea Career Decision Making® System (CDM), the Strong Interest Inventory (SII)®, or any of a wide selection of assessment tools that can help you clarify some of these issues prior to the interview stage of your job search.

## The Resume

Resume preparation has been discussed in detail, and some basic examples of various types were provided. In this section, we want to concentrate on how best to use your resume in the interview. In most cases, the employer will have seen the resume prior to the interview, and, in fact, it may well have been the quality of that resume that secured the interview opportunity.

An interview is a conversation, however, and not an exercise in reading. So, if the employer hasn't seen your resume and you have brought it along to the interview, wait until asked or until the end of the interview to offer it. Otherwise, you may find yourself staring at the back of your resume and simply answering "Yes" and "No" to a series of questions drawn from that document.

Sometimes an interviewer is not prepared and does not know or recall the contents of the resume and may use the resume to a greater or lesser degree as a "prompt" during the interview. It is for you to judge what that may indicate about the individual doing the interview or the employer. If your interviewer seems surprised by the scheduled meeting, relies on the resume to an inordinate degree, and seems otherwise unfamiliar with your background, this lack of preparation for the hiring process could well be a symptom of general management disorganization or may simply be the result of poor planning on the part of one individual. It is your responsibility as a potential employee to be aware of these signals and make your decisions accordingly.

················································

**In any event, it is perfectly acceptable for you to get the conversation back to a more interpersonal style by saying something like, "Mr. Smith, you might be interested in some recent music therapy experience I gained in an internship that is not detailed on my resume. May I tell you about it?" This can return the interview to two people talking to each other, not one reading and the other responding.**

················································

By all means, bring at least one copy of your resume to the interview. Occasionally, at the close of an interview, an interviewer will express an interest in circulating a resume to several departments, and you could then offer to provide those. Sometimes, an interview appointment provides an opportunity to meet others in the organization who may express an interest in you and your background, and it may be helpful to follow that up with a copy of your resume. Our best advice, however, is to keep it out of sight until needed or requested.

## Appearance

Although many of the absolute rules that once dominated the advice offered to job candidates about appearance have now been moderated significantly, conservative is still the watchword unless you are interviewing in a fashion-related industry. For men, conservative translates into a well-cut dark suit with appropriate tie, hosiery, and dress shirt. A wise strategy for the male job seeker looking for a good but not expensive suit would be to try the men's department of a major department store. They usually carry a good range of sizes, fabrics, and prices; offer professional sales help; provide free tailoring; and have associated departments for putting together a professional look.

For women, there is more latitude. Business suits are still popular, but they have become more feminine in color and styling with a variety of jacket and skirt lengths. In addition to suits, better quality dresses are now worn in many environments and, with the correct accessories, can be most appropriate. Company literature, professional magazines, the business section of major newspapers, and television interviews can all give clues about what is being worn in different employer environments.

Both men and women need to pay attention to issues such as hair, jewelry, and make-up; these are often what separates the candidate in appearance from the professional work force. It seems particularly difficult for the young job seeker to give up certain hair styles, eyeglass fashions, and jewelry habits, yet those can be important to the employer, who is concerned with your ability to successfully make the transition into the organization. Candidates often find the best strategy is to dress conservatively until they find employment. Once employed and familiar with the norms within your organization, you can begin to determine a look that you enjoy, works for you, and fits your organization.

Choose clothes that suit your body type, fit well, and flatter you. Feel good about the way you look! The interview day is not the best for a new hairdo, a new pair of shoes, or any other change that will distract you or cause you to be self-conscious. Arrive a bit early to avoid being rushed, and ask the receptionist to direct you to a restroom for any last-minute adjustments of hair and clothes.

## Employer Information

Whether your interview is for graduate school admission, an overseas corporate position, or a reporter position with a local newspaper, it is important to know something about the employer or the organization. Keeping in mind that the interview is relatively brief and that you will hopefully have other interviews with other organizations, it is important to keep your research in proportion. If secondary interviews are called for, you will have additional time to do further research. For the first interview, it is helpful to know the organization's mission, goals, size, scope of operations, etc. Your research may uncover recent areas of challenge or particular successes that may help to fuel the interview. Use the "Where Are These Jobs, Anyway?" section of Chapter 3, your library, and your career or guidance office to help you locate this information in the most efficient way possible. Don't be shy in asking advice of these counseling and guidance professionals on how best to spend your preparation time. With some practice, you'll soon learn how much information is enough and which kinds of information are most useful to you.

## INTERVIEW CONTENT

We've already discussed how it can help to think of the interview as an important conversation—one that, as with any conversation, you want to find pleasant and interesting and leaves you with a good feeling. But because this conversation is especially important, the information that's exchanged is critical to its success. What do you want them to know about you? What do you need to know about them? What interview technique do you need to particularly pay attention to? How do you want to manage the close of the interview? What steps will follow in the hiring process?

Except for the professional interviewer, most of us find interviewing stressful and anxiety-provoking. Developing a strategy before you begin interviewing will help you relieve some stress and anxiety. One particular strategy that has worked for many and may work for you is interviewing by objective. Before you interview, write down 3–5 goals you would like to achieve for that interview. They may be technique goals: smile a little more, have a firmer handshake, be sure to ask about the next stage in the interview process before I leave, etc. They may be content-oriented goals: find out about the company's current challenges and opportunities, be sure to speak of my recent research writing experiences or foreign travel, etc. Whatever your goals, jot down a few of them as goals for this interview.

Most people find that, in trying to achieve these few goals, their interviewing technique becomes more organized and focused. After the interview, the most common question friends and family ask is, "How did it go?" With this technique, you have an indication of whether you met *your* goals for the meeting, not just some vague idea of how it went. Chances are, if you accomplished what you wanted to, it informed the quality of the entire interview. As you continue to interview, you will want to revise your goals to continue improving your interview skills.

Now, add to the concept of the significant conversation the idea of a beginning, a middle, and a closing and you will have two thoughts that will give your interview a distinctive character. Be sure to make your introduction warm and cordial. Say your full name (and if it's a difficult-to-pronounce name, help the interviewer to pronounce it) and make certain you know your interviewer's name and how to pronounce it. Most interviews begin with some "soft talk" about the weather, chat about the candidate's trip to the interview site, national events, etc. This is done as a courtesy, to relax both you and the interviewer, to get you talking, and to generally try to defuse the atmosphere of excessive tension. Try to be yourself, engage in the conversation, and don't try to second-guess the interviewer. This is simply what it appears to be—casual conversation.

Once you and the interviewer move on to exchange more serious information in the middle part of the interview, the two most important concerns become your ability to handle challenging questions and your success at asking meaningful ones. Interviewer questions will probably fall into one of three categories: personal assessment and career direction, academic background, and knowledge of the employer. The following are some examples of questions in each category:

## Personal Assessment and Career Direction

1. How would you describe yourself?

2. What motivates you to put forth your greatest effort?

3. In what kind of work environment are you most comfortable?

4. What do you consider to be your greatest strengths and weaknesses?

5. How well do you work under pressure?

6. What qualifications do you have that make you think you will be successful in this career?

7. Will you relocate? What do you feel would be the most difficult aspect of relocating?

8. Are you willing to travel?

9. Why should I hire you?

## Academic Assessment

1. Why did you select your college or university?

2. What changes would you make at your alma mater?

3. What led you to choose your major?

4. What subjects did you like best and least? Why?

5. If you could, how would you plan your academic study differently? Why?

6. Describe your most rewarding college experience.

7. How has your college experience prepared you for this career?

8. Do you think that your grades are a good indication of your ability to succeed with this organization?

9. Do you have plans for continued study?

## Knowledge of the Employer

1. If you were hiring a graduate of your school for this position, what qualities would you look for?

2. What do you think it takes to be successful in an organization like ours?

3. In what ways do you think you can make a contribution to our organization?

4. Why did you choose to seek a position with this organization?

The interviewer wants a response to each question but is also gauging your enthusiasm, preparedness, and willingness to communicate. In each response you should provide some information about yourself that can be related to the employer's needs. A common mistake is to give too much information. Answer each question completely, but be careful not to run on too long with extensive details or examples.

## Questions about Underdeveloped Skills

Most employers interview people who have met some minimum criteria of education and experience. They interview candidates to see who they are, to learn what kind of personality they exhibit, and to get some sense of how this person might fit into the existing organization. It may be that you are asked about skills the employer hopes to find and that you have not documented. Maybe it's grant-writing experience, knowledge of the European political system, or a knowledge of the film world.

To questions about skills and experiences you don't have, answer honestly and forthrightly and try to offer some additional information about skills you do have. For example, perhaps the employer is disappointed you have no grant-writing experience. An honest answer may be as follows:

> No, unfortunately, I was never in a position to acquire those skills. I do understand something of the complexities of the grant-writing process and feel confident that my attention to detail, careful reading skills, and strong writing would make grants a wonderful challenge in a new job. I think I could get up on the learning curve quickly.

The employer hears an honest admission of lack of experience but is reassured by some specific skill details that do relate to grant writing and a confident manner that suggests enthusiasm and interest in a challenge.

For many students, questions about their possible contribution to an employer's organization can prove challenging. Because your education has probably not included specific training for a job, you need to review your academic record and select capabilities you have developed in your major that an employer can appreciate. For example, perhaps you read well and can analyze and condense what you've read into smaller, more focused pieces. That could be valuable. Or maybe you did some serious research and you know you have valuable investigative skills. Your public speaking might be highly developed and you might use visual aids appropriately and effectively. Or maybe your skill at correspondence, memos, and messages is effective. Whatever it is, you must take it out of the academic context and put it into a new, employer-friendly context so your interviewer can best judge how you could help the organization.

Exhibiting knowledge of the organization will, without a doubt, show the interviewer that you are interested enough in the available position to have done some legwork in preparation for the interview. Remember, it is not necessary to know every detail of the organization's history, but rather to have a general knowledge about why it is in business and how the industry is faring.

Sometime during the interview, generally after the midway point, you'll be asked if you have any questions for the interviewer. Your questions will tell the employer much about your attitude and your desire to understand the organization's expectations so you can compare it to your own strengths. The following are some selected questions you might want to ask:

1. What are the main responsibilities of the position?

2. What are the opportunities and challenges associated with this position?

3. Could you outline some possible career paths beginning with this position?

4. How regularly do performance evaluations occur?

5. What is the communication style of the organization? (meetings, memos, etc.)

6. Describe a typical day for me in this position.

7. What kinds of opportunities might exist for me to improve my professional skills within the organization?

8. What have been some of the interesting challenges and opportunities your organization has recently faced?

Most interviews draw to a natural closing point, so be careful not to prolong the discussion. At a signal from the interviewer, wind up your presentation, express your appreciation for the opportunity, and be sure to ask what the next stage in the process will be. When can you expect to hear from them? Will they be conducting second-tier interviews? If you're interested and haven't heard, would they mind a phone call? Be sure to collect a business card with the name and phone number of your interviewer. On your way out, you might have an opportunity to pick up organizational literature you haven't seen before.

With the right preparation—a thorough self-assessment, professional clothing, and employer information, you'll be able to set and achieve the goals you have established for the interview process.

# CHAPTER SIX

# NETWORKING OR INTERVIEWING FOLLOW-UP

Q uite often, there is a considerable time lag between interviewing for a position and being hired, or, in the case of the networker, between your phone call or letter to a possible contact and the opportunity of a meeting. This can be frustrating. "Why aren't they contacting me?" "I thought I'd get another interview, but no one has telephoned." "Am I out of the running?" You don't know what is happening.

## CONSIDER THE DIFFERING PERSPECTIVES

Of course, there is another perspective—that of the networker or hiring organization. Organizations are complex, with multiple tasks that need to be accomplished each day. Hiring is but one discrete activity that does not occur as frequently as other job assignments. The hiring process might have to take second place to other, more immediate organizational needs. Although it may be very important to you and it is certainly ultimately significant to the employer, other issues such as fiscal management, planning and product development, employer vacation periods, or financial constraints, may prevent an organization or individual within that organization from acting on your employment or your request for information as quickly as you or they would prefer.

# USE YOUR COMMUNICATION SKILLS

Good communication is essential here to resolve any anxieties, and the responsibility is on you, the job or information seeker. Too many job seekers and networkers offer as an excuse that they don't want to "bother" the organization by writing letters or calling. Let us assure you here and now, once and for all, that if you are troubling an organization by over-communicating, someone will indicate that situation to you quite clearly. If not, you can only assume you are a worthwhile prospect and the employer appreciates being reminded of your availability and interest in them. Let's look at follow-up practices in both the job interview process and the networking situation separately.

# FOLLOWING UP ON THE EMPLOYMENT INTERVIEW

A brief thank-you note following an interview is an excellent and polite way to begin a series of follow-up communications with a potential employer with whom you have interviewed and want to remain in touch. It should be just that—a thank-you for a good meeting. If you failed to mention some fact or experience during your interview that you think might add to your candidacy, you may use this note to do that. However, this should be essentially a note whose overall tone is appreciative and, if appropriate, indicative of a continuing interest in pursuing any opportunity that may exist with that organization. It is one of the few pieces of business correspondence that may be handwritten, but always use plain, good-quality, monarch-size paper.

If, however, at this point you are no longer interested in the employer, the thank-you note is an appropriate time to indicate that. You are under no obligation to identify any reason for not continuing to pursue employment with that organization, but if you are so inclined to indicate your professional reasons (pursuing other employers more akin to your interests, looking for greater income production than this employer can provide, a different geographic location than is available, etc.), you certainly may. It should not be written with an eye to negotiation, for it will not be interpreted as such.

As part of your interview closing, you should have taken the initiative to establish lines of communication for continuing information about your candidacy. If you asked permission to telephone, wait a week following your thank-you note, then telephone your contact simply to inquire how things are progressing on your employment status. The feedback you receive here should be taken at face value. If your interviewer simply has no information, he or she will tell you so and indicate whether you should call again and when. Don't be discouraged if this should continue over some period of time.

If during this time something occurs that you think improves or changes your candidacy (some new qualification or experience you may have had), including any offers from other organizations, by all means telephone or write to inform the employer about this. In the case of an offer from a competing but less desirable or equally desirable organization, telephone your contact, explain what has happened, express your real interest in the organization, and inquire whether some determination on your employment might be made before you must respond to this other offer. If the organization is truly interested in you, they may be moved to make a decision about your candidacy. Equally possible is the scenario in which they are not yet ready to make a decision and so advise you to take the offer that has been presented. Again, you have no ethical alternative but to deal with the information presented in a straightforward manner.

When accepting other employment, be sure to contact any employers still actively considering you and inform them of your new job. Thank them graciously for their consideration. There are many other job seekers out there just like you who will benefit from having their candidacy improved when others bow out of the race. Who knows, you might, at some future time, have occasion to interact professionally with one of the organizations with whom you sought employment. How embarrassing to have someone remember you as the candidate who failed to notify them of taking a job elsewhere!

In all of your follow-up communications, keep good notes of who you spoke with, when you called, and any instructions that were given about return communications. This will prevent any misunderstandings and provide you with good records of what has transpired.

## FOLLOWING UP ON THE NETWORK CONTACT

Far more common than the forgotten follow-up after an interview is the situation where a good network contact is allowed to lapse. Good communications are the essence of a network, and follow-up is not so much a matter of courtesy here as it is a necessity. In networking for job information and contacts, you are the active network link. Without you, and without continual contact from you, there is no network. You and your need for employment is often the only shared element between members of the network. Because network contacts were made regardless of the availability of any particular employment, it is incumbent upon the job seeker, if not simple common sense, that unless you stay in regular communication with the network, you will not be available for consideration should some job become available in the future.

This brings up the issue of responsibility, which is likewise very clear. The job seeker initiates network contacts and is responsible for maintaining those contacts; therefore, the entire responsibility for the network belongs with him or her. This becomes patently obvious if the network is left unattended. It very shortly falls out of existence, as it cannot survive without careful attention by the networker.

A variety of ways are open to you to keep the lines of communication open and to attempt to interest the network in you as a possible employee. You are limited only by your own enthusiasm for members of the network and your creativity. However, you as a networker are well advised to keep good records of whom you have met and spoken with in each organization. Be sure to send thank-you notes to anyone who has spent any time with you, be it a quick tour of a department or a sit-down informational interview. All of these communications should, in addition to their ostensible reason, add some information about you and your particular combination of strengths and attributes.

You can contact your network at any time to convey continued interest, to comment on some recent article you came across concerning an organization, to add information about your training or changes in your qualifications, to ask advice or seek guidance in your job search, or to request referrals to other possible network opportunities. Sometimes just a simple note to network members reminding them of your job search, indicating that you have been using their advice, and noting that you are still actively pursuing leads and hope to continue to interact with them is enough to keep communications alive.

Because networks have been abused in the past, it's important that your conduct be above reproach. Networks are exploratory options, they are not back-door access to employers. The network works best for someone who is exploring a new industry or making a transition into a new area of employment and who needs to find information or to alert people to their search activity. Always be candid and direct with contacts in expressing the purpose of your call or letter and your interest in their help or information about their organization. In follow-up contacts, keep the tone professional and direct. Your honesty will be appreciated, and people will respond as best they can if your qualifications appear to meet their forthcoming needs. The network does not owe you anything, and that tone should be clear to each person you meet.

## FEEDBACK FROM FOLLOW-UPS

A network contact may prove to be miscalculated. Perhaps you were referred to someone and it became clear that your goals and their particular needs did not make a good match. Or the network contact may simply not be in a position to provide you with the information you are seeking. Or in some unfortunate situations, the contact may become annoyed by being contacted for this purpose. In such a situation, many job seekers simply say "Thank you" and move on.

If the contact is simply not the right contact, but the individual you are speaking with is not annoyed by the call, it might be a better tactic to express regret that the contact was misplaced and then express to the contact what you are seeking and ask for their advice or possible suggestions as to a next step. The more people who are aware you are seeking employment, the better your chances of connecting, and that is the purpose of a network. Most people in a profession have excellent knowledge of their field and varying amounts of expertise on areas near to or tangent to their own. Use their expertise and seek some guidance before you dissolve the contact. You may be pleasantly surprised.

Occasionally, networkers will express the feeling that they have done as much as they can or provided all the information that is available to them. This may be a cue that they would like to be released from your network. Be alert to such attempts to terminate, graciously thank the individual by letter, and move on in your network development. A network is always changing, adding and losing members, and you want the network to be composed of only those who are actively interested in supporting your interests.

## A Final Point on Networking for Music Majors

In any of the settings a music major might consider as a potential place to work, your contacts will be critically evaluating all of your written and oral communications. This should serve to emphasize the importance of the quality of your interactions with people in a position to help you in your job search.

In your telephone communications, interview presentation, and follow-up correspondence, your warmth, style, and personality as evidenced in your spoken and written use of English will be part of the portfolio of impressions you create just as much as your music ability.

# CHAPTER SEVEN

# JOB OFFER CONSIDERATIONS

**f**or many recent college graduates, the thrill of their first job and, for some, the most substantial regular income they have ever earned seems an excess of good fortune coming at once. To question that first income or be critical in any way of the conditions of employment at the time of the initial offer seems like looking a gift horse in the mouth. It doesn't seem to occur to many new hires even to attempt to negotiate any aspect of their first job. And, as many employers who deal with entry-level jobs for recent college graduates will readily confirm, the reality is that there simply isn't much movement in salary available to these new college recruits. The entry-level hire generally does not have an employment track record on a professional level to provide any leverage for negotiation. Real negotiations on salary, benefits, retirement provisions, etc., come to those with significant employment records at higher income levels.

Of course, the job offer is more than just money. It can be comprised of geographic assignment, duties and responsibilities, training, benefits, health and medical insurance, educational assistance, car allowance or company vehicle, and a host of other items. All of this is generally detailed in the formal letter that presents the final job offer. In most cases, this is a follow-up to a personal phone call from the employer representative who has been principally responsible for your hiring process.

That initial telephone offer is certainly binding as a verbal agreement, but most firms follow up with a detailed letter outlining the most significant parts of your employment contract. You may certainly choose to respond immediately at the time of the telephone offer (which would be considered a binding oral contract), but you will also be required to formally answer the letter of offer with a letter of acceptance, restating the salient elements of the employer's description of your position, salary, and benefits. This ensures that both parties are clear on the terms and conditions of employment and remuneration and any other outstanding aspects of the job offer.

## Is This the Job You Want?

Most new employees will write this letter of acceptance back, glad to be in the position to accept employment. If you've worked hard to get the offer, and the job market is tight, other offers may not be in sight, so you will say "Yes, I accept!" What is important here is that the job offer you accept be one that does fit your particular needs, values, and interests as you've outlined them in your self-assessment process. Moreover, it should be a job that will not only use your skills and education, but also challenge you to develop new skills and talents.

Jobs are sometimes accepted too hastily, for the wrong reasons and without proper scrutiny by the applicant. For example, an individual might readily accept a sales job only to find the continual rejection by potential clients unendurable. An office worker might realize within weeks the constraints of a desk job and yearn for more activity. Employment is an important part of our lives. It is, for most of our adult lives, our most continuous productive activity. We want to make good choices based on the right criteria.

If you have a low tolerance for risk, a job based on commission will certainly be very anxiety provoking. If being near your family is important, issues of relocation could present a decision crisis for you. If you're an adventurous person, a job with frequent travel would provide needed excitement and be very desirable. The importance of income, the need to continue your education, your personal health situation—all of these have an impact on whether the job you are considering will ultimately meet your needs. Unless you've spent some time understanding and thinking about these issues, it will be difficult to evaluate offers you do receive.

More importantly, if you make a decision that you cannot tolerate and feel you must leave that job, you will then have both unemployment and self-esteem issues to contend with. These will combine to make the next job search tough going, indeed. So make your acceptance a carefully considered decision.

## Negotiating Your Offer

It may be that there is some aspect of your job offer that is not particularly attractive to you. Perhaps there is no relocation allotment to help you move your possessions and this presents some financial hardship for you. It may be that the medical and health insurance is less than you had hoped. Your initial assignment may be different than you expected, either in its location or in the duties and responsibilities that comprise it. Or it may simply be that the salary is less than you anticipated. Other considerations may be your official starting date of employment, vacation time, evening hours, dates of training programs or schools, etc.

If you are considering not accepting the job because of some item or items in the job offer "package" that do not meet your needs, you should know that most employers emphatically wish that you would bring that issue to their attention. It may be that the employer can alter it to make the offer more agreeable for you. In some cases, it cannot be changed. In any event, the employer would generally like to have the opportunity to try to remedy a difficulty rather than risk losing a good potential employee over an issue that might have been resolved. After all, they have spent time and funds in securing your services, and they certainly deserve an opportunity to resolve any possible differences.

Honesty is the best approach in discussing any objections or uneasiness you might have over the employer's offer. Having received your formal offer in writing, contact your employer representative and indicate your particular dissatisfaction in a straightforward manner. For example, you might explain that, while very interested in being employed by this organization, the salary (or any other benefit) is less than you have determined you require. State the terms you do need, and listen to the response. You may be asked to put this in writing, or you may be asked to hold off until the firm can decide on a response. If you are dealing with a senior representative of the organization, one who has been involved in hiring for some time, you may get an immediate response or a solid indication of possible outcomes.

Perhaps the issue is one of relocation. Your initial assignment is in the Midwest, and because you had indicated a strong West Coast preference, you are surprised at the actual assignment. You might simply indicate that, while you understand the need for the company to assign you based on its needs, you are disappointed and had hoped to be placed on the West Coast. You could inquire if that were still possible and, if not, would it be reasonable to expect a West Coast relocation in the future.

If your request is presented in a reasonable way, the employer will not see this as jeopardizing your offer. If they can agree to your proposal, they will. If not, they will simply tell you so, and you may choose to continue your candidacy with them or remove yourself from consideration as a possible employee. The choice will be up to you.

Some firms will adjust benefits within their parameters to meet the candidate's need if at all possible. If a candidate requires a relocation cost allowance, he or she may be asked to forgo tuition benefits for the first year to accomplish this adjustment. An increase in life insurance may be adjusted by some other benefit trade-off; perhaps a family dental plan is not needed. In these decisions, you are called upon, sometimes under time pressure, to know how you value these issues and how important each is to you.

Many employers find they are more comfortable negotiating for candidates who have unique qualifications or who bring especially needed expertise to the organization. Employers hiring large numbers of entry-level college graduates may be far more reluctant to accommodate any changes in offer conditions. They are well supplied with candidates with similar education and experience, so that if rejected by one candidate, they can draw new candidates from an ample labor pool.

## COMPARING OFFERS

With only about 40 percent of recent college graduates employed three months after graduation, many graduates do not get to enjoy the experience of entertaining more than one offer at a time. The conditions of the economy, the job seekers' particular geographic job market, and their own needs and demands for certain employment conditions may not provide more than one offer at a time. Some job seekers may feel that no reasonable offer should go unaccepted, for the simple fear there won't be another.

In a tough job market, or if the job you seek is not widely available, or when your job search goes on too long and becomes difficult to sustain financially and emotionally, it may be necessary to accept an offer. The alternative is continued unemployment. Even here, when you feel you don't have a choice, you can at least understand that in accepting this particular offer, there may be limitations and conditions you don't appreciate. At the time of acceptance, there were no other alternatives, but the new employee can begin to use that position to gain the experience and talent to move toward a more attractive position.

Sometimes, however, more than one offer is received at one time, and the candidate has the luxury of choice. If the job seeker knows what he or she wants and has done the necessary self-assessment honestly and thoroughly, it may be clear that one of the offers conforms more closely to those expressed wants and needs.

However, if, as so often happens, the offers are similar in terms of conditions and salary, the question then becomes which organization might provide the necessary climate, opportunities, and advantages for your professional development and growth. This is the time when solid employer research and astute questioning during the interviews really pays off. How much did you learn about the employer through your own research and skillful questioning? When the interviewer asked during the interview, "Now, I'm sure you must have many questions?" did you ask the kinds of questions that would help resolve a choice between one organization and another? Just as an employer must decide among numerous applicants, so must the applicant learn to assess the potential employer. Both are partners in the job search.

## RENEGING ON AN OFFER

An especially disturbing occurrence for employers and career counseling professionals is when a student formally (either orally or by written contract) accepts employment with one organization and later reneges on the agreement and goes with another employer.

There are all kinds of rationalizations offered for this unethical behavior. None of them satisfies. The sad irony is that what the job seeker is willing to do to the employer—make a promise and then break it—he or she would be outraged to have done to them—have the job offer pulled. It is a very bad way to begin a career. It suggests the individual has not taken the time to do the necessary self-assessment and self-awareness exercises to think and judge critically. The new offer taken may, in fact, be no better or worse than the one refused. Job candidates should be aware that there have been incidents of legal action following job candidates reneging on an offer. This adds a very sour note to what should be a harmonious beginning of a lifelong adventure.

# CHAPTER EIGHT

# THE GRADUATE SCHOOL CHOICE

The reasons for continuing one's education in graduate school can be as varied and unique as the individuals electing this course of action. Many continue their studies at an advanced level because they simply find it difficult to end the educational process. They love what they are learning and want to learn more and continue their academic exploration.

Studying a particular subject in great depth—such as techniques used by eighteenth century composers—and thinking, studying, researching, and writing critically on what others have discovered can provide excitement, challenge, and serious work. Some music majors have loved this aspect of their academic work and want to continue that activity.

Others go on to graduate school for purely practical reasons: they have examined employment prospects in their field of study, and all indications are that a graduate degree is requisite. If you have earned a BA in music as a stepping stone to a career in music library work, for example, going on for further training becomes mandatory. As a BA level music major, you realize you cannot move above entry level without a master's degree or even a doctorate. A review of jobs in different areas will suggest that at least a master's degree is important to be competitive. Alumni who are working in entertainment, education, the media, in museums, in libraries, or in writing and publishing can be a good resource as to what degree level the fields are hiring. Ask your college career office for some alumni names and give them a telephone call. Prepare some questions on specific job prospects in their field at each degree level. A thorough examination of the marketplace and talking to employers and professors will give you a sense of the scope of employment for a bachelor's degree, master's degree, or doctorate.

College teaching will require an advanced degree. Your job prospects might also demand specialization in an additional field (electronics, broadcasting, etc.). Libraries and other settings may well put a premium on the advanced degree because the market is oversupplied and the employer can afford to make this demand, or because the advanced training and research are requirements to function in the job.

## Consider Your Motives

The answer to the question of "Why graduate school?" is a personal one for each applicant. Nevertheless, it is important to consider your motives carefully. Graduate school involves additional time out of the employment market, a high degree of critical evaluation, significant autonomy as you pursue your studies, and considerable financial expenditure. For some students in doctoral programs, there may be additional life choice issues, such as relationships, marriage, and parenthood that may present real challenges while in a program of study. You would be well advised to consider the following questions as you think about your decision to continue your studies.

### Are You Postponing Some Tough Decisions by Going to School?

Graduate school is not a place to go to avoid life's problems. There is intense competition for graduate school slots and for the fellowships, scholarships, and financial aid available. This competition means extensive interviewing, resume submission, and essay writing that rivals corporate recruitment. Likewise, the graduate school process is a mentored one in which faculty stay aware of and involved in the academic progress of their students and continually challenge the quality of their work. Many graduate students are called upon to participate in teaching and professional writing and research as well.

In other words, this is no place to hide from the spotlight. Graduate students work very hard and much is demanded of them individually. If you elect to go to graduate school to avoid the stresses and strains of the "real world," you will find no safe place in higher academics. Vivid accounts, both fiction and nonfiction, have depicted quite accurately the personal and professional demands of graduate school work.

The selection of graduate studies as a career option should be a positive choice—something you *want* to do. It shouldn't be selected as an escape from other, less attractive or more challenging options, nor should it be selected as the option of last resort (i.e., "I can't do anything else; I'd better just stay in school"). If you're in some doubt about the strength of your reasoning about continuing in school, discuss the issues with a career counselor. Together you can clarify your reasoning, and you'll get some sound feedback on what you're about to undertake.

On the other hand, staying on in graduate school because of a particularly poor employment market and a lack of jobs at entry-level positions has proven to be an effective "stalling" strategy. If you can afford it, pursuing a graduate degree immediately after your undergraduate education gives you a year or two to "wait out" a difficult economic climate while at the same time acquiring a potentially valuable credential.

## Have You Done Some "Hands-on" Reality Testing?

There are experiential options available to give some reality to your decision-making process about graduate school. Internships or work in the field can give you a good idea about employment demands, conditions, and atmosphere.

Perhaps, as a music major, you're considering a graduate program in music education with an eye to university teaching. Begin with your own college professors and ask them to talk to you about their own educational and career paths to their current treaching posts. They can also talk to you about the time they spend outside the classroom, in research activities or in departmental meetings dealing with faculty and budget concerns.

Even hearing the experience of only one professor, you have a stronger concept of the pace of the job, interaction with colleagues, subject matter, and pressure to do research and publish results. Talking to people and asking questions is invaluable as an exercise to help you better understand the objective of your graduate study.

For music majors especially, the opportunity to do this kind of reality testing is invaluable. It demonstrates far more authoritatively than any other method what your real-world skills are, how they can be put to use, and what aspect of your academic preparation you rely on. It has been well documented that music majors do well in occupations once they identify them. Internships and co-op experiences speed that process up and prevent the frustrating and expensive process of investigation many graduates begin only after graduation.

........................................................

## Do You Need an Advanced Degree to Work in Your Field?

Certainly there are fields such as law, psychiatry, medicine, and college teaching that demand advanced degrees. Is the field of employment you're considering one that also puts a premium on an advanced degree? You may be surprised. Read the want ads in a number of major Sunday newspapers for positions you would enjoy. How many of those require an advanced degree?

Retailing, for example, has always put a premium on what people can do, rather than how much education they have had. Successful people in retailing come from all academic preparations. A Ph.D. in English may bring only prestige to the individual employed as a magazine researcher. It may not bring a more senior position or better pay. In fact, it may disqualify you for some jobs because an employer might believe you will be unhappy to be overqualified for a particular position. Or your motives in applying for the work may be misconstrued, and the employer might think you will only be working at this level until something better comes along. None of this may be true for you, but it comes about because you are working outside of the usual territory for that degree level.

When economic times are especially difficult, we tend to see stories featured about individuals with advanced degrees doing what is considered unsuitable work, such as the Ph.D. in English driving a cab or the Ph.D. in chemistry waiting tables. Actually, this is not particularly surprising when you consider that as your degree level advances, the job market narrows appreciably. At any one time, regardless of economic circumstances, there are only so many jobs for your particular level of expertise. If you cannot find employment for your advanced degree level, chances are you will be considered suspect for many other kinds of employment and may be forced into temporary work far removed from your original intention.

Before making an important decision such as graduate study, learn your options and carefully consider what you want to do with your advanced degree. Ask yourself whether it is reasonable to think you can achieve your goals. Will there be jobs when you graduate? Where will they be? What will they pay? How competitive will the market be at that time, based on current predictions?

If you're uncertain about the degree requirements for the fields you're interested in, you should check a publication such as the U.S. Department of Labor's *Occupational Outlook Handbook*. Each entry has a section on training and other qualifications that will indicate clearly what the minimum educational requirement is for employment, what degree is the standard, and what employment may be possible without the required credential.

For example, for physicists and astronomers, a doctoral degree in physics or a closely related field is essential. Certainly this is the degree of choice in academic institutions. However, the *Occupational Outlook Handbook* also indicates what kinds of employment may be available to individuals holding a master's or even a bachelor's degree in physics.

## Have You Compared Your Expectations of What Graduate School Will Do for You with What It Has Done for Alumni of the Program You're Considering?

Most colleges and universities perform some kind of postgraduate survey of their students to ascertain where they are employed, what additional education they have received, and what levels of salary they are enjoying. Ask to see this information either from the university you are considering applying to or from your own alma mater, especially if it has a similar graduate program. Such surveys often reveal surprises about occupational decisions, salaries, and work satisfaction. This information may affect your decision.

The value of self-assessment (the process of examining and making decisions about your own hierarchy of values and goals) is especially important in this process of analyzing the desirability of possible career paths involving graduate education. Sometimes a job requiring advanced education seems to hold real promise but is disappointing in salary potential or numbers of opportunities available. Certainly, it is better to research this information before embarking on a program of graduate studies. It may not change your mind about your decision, but by becoming better informed about your choice, you become better prepared for your future.

## Have You Talked with People in Your Field to Explore What You Might Be Doing after Graduate School?

In pursuing your undergraduate degree, you will have come into contact with many individuals trained in the field you are considering. You might also have the opportunity to attend professional conferences, workshops, seminars, and job fairs where you can expand your network of contacts. Talk to them all! Find out about their individual career paths, discuss your own plans and hopes, and get their feedback on the reality of your expectations, and heed their advice about your prospects. Each will have a unique tale to tell, and each will bring a different perspective on the current marketplace for the credentials you are seeking. Talking to enough people will make you an expert on what's out there.

## Are You Excited by the Idea of Studying the Particular Field You Have in Mind?

This question may be the most important one of all. If you are going to spend several years in advanced study, perhaps engendering some debt or postponing some life-style decisions for an advanced degree, you simply ought to enjoy what you're doing. Examine your work in the discipline so far. Has it been fun? Have you found yourself exploring various paths of thought? Do you read in your area for fun? Do you enjoy talking about it, thinking about it, and sharing it with others? Advanced degrees often are the beginning of a lifetime's involvement with a particular subject. Choose carefully a field that will hold your interest and your enthusiasm.

It is fairly obvious by now that we think you should give some careful thought to your decision and take some action. If nothing else, do the following:

❑ Talk and question (remember to listen!)

❑ Reality-test

❑ Soul-search by yourself or with a person you trust

# FINDING THE RIGHT PROGRAM FOR YOU: SOME CONSIDERATIONS

There are several important factors in coming to a sound decision about the right graduate program for you. You'll want to begin by locating institutions that offer appropriate programs, examining each of these programs and their requirements, undertaking the application process by obtaining catalogs and application materials, visiting campuses if possible, arranging for letters of recommendation, writing your application statement, and finally following up on your applications.

## Locate Institutions with Appropriate Programs

Once you decide on a particular advanced degree, it's important to develop a list of schools offering such a degree program. Perhaps the best source of graduate program information are Peterson's *Guides to Graduate Study*. Use these guides to build your list. In addition, you may want to consult the College Board's *Index of Majors and Graduate Degrees,* which will help you find graduate programs offering the degree you seek. It is indexed by academic major and then categorized by state.

Now, this may be a considerable list. You may want to narrow the choices down further by a number of criteria: tuition, availability of financial aid, public versus private institutions, U.S. versus international institutions, size of student body, size of faculty, application fee (this varies by school; most fall within the $10–$75 range), and geographic location. This is only a partial list; you will have your own important considerations. Perhaps you are an avid scuba diver and you find it unrealistic to think you could pursue graduate study for a number of years without being able to ocean dive from time to time. Good! That's a decision and it's honest. Now, how far from the ocean is too far, and what schools meet your other needs? In any case, and according to your own criteria, begin to build a reasonable list of graduate schools that you are willing to spend the time investigating.

## Examine the Degree Programs and Their Requirements

Once you've determined the criteria by which you want to develop a list of graduate schools, you can begin to examine the degree program requirements, faculty composition, and institutional research orientation. Again, using a resource such as Peterson's *Guides to Graduate Study* can reveal an amazingly rich level of material by which to judge your possible selections.

In addition to degree programs and degree requirements, entries will include information about application fees, entrance test requirements, tuition, percentage of applicants accepted, numbers of applicants receiving financial aid, gender breakdown of students, numbers of full- and part-time faculty, and often gender breakdown of faculty as well. Numbers graduating in each program and research orientations of departments are also included in some entries. There is information on graduate housing, student services, and library, research, and computer facilities. A contact person, phone number, and address are also standard pieces of information in these listings. In addition to the standard entries, some schools pay an additional fee to place full-page, more detailed program descriptions. The location of such a display ad, if present, would be indicated at the end of the standard entry.

It can be helpful to draw up a chart and enter relevant information about each school you are considering in order to have a ready reference on points of information that are important to you.

## Undertake the Application Process

**The Catalog.**    Once you've decided on a selection of schools, send for catalogs and applications. It is important to note here that these materials might take many weeks to arrive. Consequently, if you need the materials quickly, it might be best to telephone and explain your situation to see whether the process can be speeded up for you. Also, check a local college or university library, which might have current and complete college catalogs in a microfiche collection. These microfiche copies can provide you with helpful information while you wait for your own copy of the graduate school catalog or bulletin to arrive.

When you receive your catalogs, give them a careful reading and make notes of issues you might want to discuss on the telephone or in a personal interview, if that's possible. Does the course selection have the depth you had hoped for?

........................................

**If you are interested in graduate work in music history, for example, in addition to classic courses such as theory or composition, consider the availability of colloquiums, directed research opportunities, and specialized seminars.**

........................................

What is the ratio of faculty to the required number of courses for your degree? How often will you encounter the same faculty member as an instructor?

If, for example, your program offers a practicum or off-campus experience, who arranges this? Does the graduate school select a site and place you there, or is it your responsibility? What are the professional affiliations of the faculty? Does the program merit any outside professional endorsement or accreditation?

Critically evaluate the catalogs of each of the programs you are considering. List any questions you have and ask current or former teachers and colleagues for their impressions as well.

**The Application.** Preview each application thoroughly to determine what you need to provide in the way of letters of recommendation, transcripts from undergraduate schools or any previous graduate work, and personal essays that may be required. Make a notation for each application of what you need to complete that document.

Additionally, you'll want to determine entrance testing requirements for each institution and immediately arrange to complete your test registration. For example, the Graduate Record Exam (GRE) and the Graduate Management Admission Test (GMAT) each have 3–4 weeks between the last registration date and the test date. Your local college career office should be able to provide you with test registration booklets, sample test materials, information on test sites and dates, and independent test review materials that might be available commercially.

## Visit the Campus If Possible

If time and finances allow, a visit, interview, and tour can help make your decision easier. You can develop a sense of the student body, meet some of the faculty, and hear up-to-date information on resources and the curriculum. You will have a brief opportunity to "try out" the surroundings to see if they fit your needs. After all, it will be home for a while. If a visit is not possible but you have questions, don't hesitate to call and speak with the dean of the graduate school. Most are more than happy to talk to candidates and want them to have the answers they seek. Graduate school admission is a very personal and individual process.

## Arrange for Letters of Recommendation

This is also the time to begin to assemble a group of individuals who will support your candidacy as a graduate student by writing letters of recommendation or completing recommendation forms. Some schools will ask you to provide letters of recommendation to be included with your application or sent directly to the school by the recommender. Other graduate programs will provide a recommendation form that must be completed by the recommender. These graduate school forms vary greatly in the amount of space provided for a written recommendation. So that you can use letters as you need to, ask your recommenders to address their letters "To Whom It May Concern," unless one of your recommenders has a particular connection to one of your graduate schools or knows an official at the school.

Choose recommenders who can speak authoritatively about the criteria important to selection officials at your graduate school. In other words, choose recommenders who can write about your grasp of the literature in your field of study, your ability to write and speak effectively, your class performance, and your demonstrated interest in the field outside of class. Other characteristics that graduate schools are interested in assessing include your emotional maturity, leadership ability, breadth of general knowledge, intellectual ability, motivation, perseverance, and ability to engage in independent inquiry.

When requesting recommendations, it's especially helpful to put the request in writing. Explain your graduate school intentions and express some of your thoughts about graduate school and your appreciation for their support. Don't be shy about "prompting" your recommenders with some suggestions of what you would appreciate being included in their comments. Most recommenders will find this direction helpful and will want to produce a statement of support that you can both stand behind. Consequently, if your interaction with one recommender was especially focused on research projects, he or she might be best able to speak of those skills and your critical thinking ability. Another recommender may have good comments to make about your public presentation skills.

Give your recommenders plenty of lead time in which to complete your recommendation, and set a date by which they should respond. If they fail to meet your deadline, be prepared to make a polite call or visit to inquire if they need more information or if there is anything you can do to move the process along.

Whether or not you are providing a graduate school form or asking for an original letter to be mailed, be sure to provide an envelope and postage if the recommender must mail the form or letter directly to the graduate school.

Each recommendation you request should provide a different piece of information about you for the selection committee. It might be pleasant for letters of recommendation to say that you are a fine, upstanding individual, but a selection committee for graduate school will require specific information. Each recommender has had a unique relationship with you, and their letters should reflect that. Think of each letter as helping to build a more complete portrait of you as a potential graduate student.

## Write Your Application Statement

······························································

For the music major, the application and personal essay should be a welcome opportunity to express your deep interest in pursuing graduate study. Your understanding of the challenges ahead, your commitment to the work involved, and your expressed self-awareness will weigh heavily in the decision process of the graduate school admissions committee.

······························································

An excellent source to help in thinking about writing this essay is *How to Write a Winning Personal Statement for Graduate and Professional School* by Richard J. Stelzer. It has been written from the perspective of what graduate school selection committees are looking for when they read these essays. It provides helpful tips to keep your essay targeted on the kinds of issues and criteria that are important to selection committees and that provide them with the kind of information they can best utilize in making their decision.

## Follow Up on Your Applications

After you have finished each application and mailed it along with your transcript requests and letters of recommendation, be sure to follow up on the progress of your file. For example, call the graduate school administrative staff to see whether your transcripts have arrived. If the school required your recommenders to fill out a specific recommendation form that had to be mailed directly to the school, you will want to ensure that they have all arrived in good time for the processing of your application. It is your responsibility to make certain that all required information is received by the institution.

# Researching Financial Aid Sources, Scholarships, and Fellowships

Financial aid information is available from each school, so be sure to request it when you call for a catalog and application materials. There will be several lengthy forms to complete, and these will vary by school, type of school (public versus private), and state. Be sure to note the deadline dates for these important forms.

There are many excellent resources available to help you explore all of your financial aid options. Visit your college career office or local public library to find out about the range of materials available. Two excellent resources include Peterson's *Grants for Graduate Students* and the Foundation Center's *Foundation Grants to Individuals*. These types of resources generally contain information that can be accessed by indexes including field of study, specific eligibility requirements, administering agency, and geographic focus.

# Evaluating Acceptances

If you apply to and are accepted at more than one school, it is time to return to your initial research and self-assessment to evaluate your options and select the program that will best help you achieve the goals you set for pursuing graduate study. You'll want to choose a program that will allow you to complete your studies in a timely and cost-effective way. This may be a good time to get additional feedback from professors and career professionals who are familiar with your interests and plans. Ultimately, the decision is yours, so be sure you get answers to all the questions you can think of.

# Some Notes about Rejection

Each graduate school is searching for applicants who appear to have the qualifications necessary to succeed in its program. Applications are evaluated on a combination of undergraduate grade point average, strength of letters of recommendation, standardized test scores, and personal statements written for the application.

A carelessly completed application is one reason many applicants are denied admission to a graduate program. To avoid this type of needless rejection, be sure to carefully and completely answer all appropriate questions on the application form, focus your personal statement given the instructions provided, and submit your materials well in advance of the deadline. Remember that your test scores and recommendations are considered a part of your application, so they must also be received by the deadline.

If you are rejected by a school that especially interests you, you may want to contact the dean of graduate studies to discuss the strengths and weaknesses of your application. Information provided by the dean will be useful in reapplying to the program or applying to other, similar programs.

# PART TWO

# THE CAREER PATHS

# CHAPTER NINE

# INTRODUCTION TO THE MUSIC CAREER PATHS

*Music is the universal language of mankind.*

**Longfellow,**
*Outre-Mer*

How can you best express your love for music? You must examine your skills, abilities, strengths, weaknesses, standards, priorities, goals, dreams, and hopes to determine which aspect of the world of music is most appealing and most possible for you.

Then ask yourself the following questions:

What kinds of music do I enjoy most?

Do I want a 9-to-5 job?

Do I mind traveling?

Do I like to be the center of attention?

Would I prefer to be unseen and unidentified?

Am I strong in the area of creating something new?

Do I like working in a group situation?

Am I happier working alone?

Do I mind working long hours?

Do I like the idea of being my own boss?

Am I good at passing information on to others?

Do I enjoy working with adults or children?

What type of music do I like best?

Do I want to specialize in one kind of music or several?

Would I prefer doing a variety of things—or only one?

Do I prefer to work primarily with my hands or my mind?

Answering these questions will give you a point from which to start.

## IN THIS BOOK

Though the book does not provide information about every career in the world of music, the chapters that follow offer a multitude of information about many careers in this field. There is one element they all have in common: All provide you with the opportunity to express your love for music.

The seven career paths described in this book include:

1. Performing

2. Behind the Scenes

3. The Business of Music

4. Creating Music

5. Teaching Music

6. Music Retailing, Wholesaling, and Repair

7. Other Music Careers

Music is a very wide field that provides many opportunities for those willing to prepare themselves and work hard to achieve success. Read on to determine which area of music appeals to you most, and take the necessary steps to fulfill your dream.

*Far and away the best
prize that life offers is the
chance to work hard at work
worth doing.*

**Theodore Roosevelt**

# CHAPTER TEN

# PATH 1: PERFORMING

*After silence,*
*that which comes*
*nearest to expressing*
*the inexpressible*
*is music.*

**Aldous Huxley**
from *Music at Night*

**Excellent voices wanted!** For commercials, cartoons, etc. Including singing. The field offers excellent compensation for the right people. Experience not always required. Please call: (667) 555-1188

**Music and Education Director.** Village Church seeks a Children's Music and Education Director. Ten-month year. Degree in music and/or education with proficiency in music required. Call (774) 555-1122 or send resume to 226 Bird Drive.

**Singers Needed.** The Southeast Choral Society needs tenor and bass singers with previous choral experience to sing in its two remaining season's concerts. Rehearsals for the March concert are held on Mondays, at the River Road Community Church, 555 Bride Drive. Please see Jane Michaels.

continued

Do any of the real want ads shown on the previous page sound like something you would yearn to be a part of? Are music and performing at the core of your very being—something from which you derive great enjoyment? Has music always been a special part of your life? Are you one of the people who has always longed to appear before audiences? Did you ever stand in front of your mirror and pretend your hair brush was a microphone? Did you play your musical instruments for friends, family, pets—virtually anyone who would listen? Many aspiring performers have done just that!

Some individuals succeed early in life—Lorin Maazel conducted two major symphony orchestras before the age of thirteen and went on to enjoy a successful career as an adult conductor. Yehudi Menuhin made his violin debut at seven. Sergei Prokofiev was already performing as a pianist at the ripe old age of six and composed an opera at the age of nine. His *Peter and the Wolf* has been a source of entertainment for both children and adults for many decades.

No matter how old you are, the following chapter will provide you with the information you need to pursue a career in performing music.

## DEFINITION OF THE CAREER PATH

Successful professional musicians are artists who express themselves through their music by conducting, playing instruments, or singing (or both). Through their talent, many years of hard work, initiative, and perhaps a lucky break, they make a living and entertain audiences doing what they love most, making music.

## CAREER CHOICES IN PERFORMING

### Musician

The number of musicians who perform in the United States is estimated to be about 256,000. Included are those who play in any one of 39 regional, 90 metropolitan, or 30 major symphony orchestras. (Large orchestras employ from 85 to 105 musicians while smaller ones employ 60 to 75 players.) Also counted are those who are a part of hundreds of small orchestras, symphony orchestras, pop and jazz groups, and those who broadcast or record.

Instrumental musicians may play a variety of musical instruments in an orchestra, popular band, marching band, military band, concert band, symphony, dance band, rock group, or jazz group and may specialize in string, brass, woodwind, percussion instruments, or electronic synthesizers. A large percentage of musicians are proficient in playing several related instruments, such as the flute and clarinet. Those who are very talented have the option to perform as soloists.

Rehearsing and performing take up much of the musician's time and energy. In addition, musicians, especially those without agents, may need to perform a number of other routine tasks: making reservations; keeping track of auditions and/or recordings; arranging for sound effects, amplifiers, and other equipment to enhance performances; designing lighting, costuming, and makeup; bookkeeping; setting up advertising, concerts, tickets, programs, and contracts. In addition, it is necessary for musicians to plan the sequence of the numbers to be performed and/or arrange their music according to the conductor's instructions before performances.

Musicians must also keep their instruments clean, polished, tuned, and in proper working order. In addition, they are expected to attend meetings with agents, employers, and conductors or directors to discuss contracts, engagements, and any other business activities.

Performing musicians encompass a wide variety of careers. Following are just a few of the possibilities:

**Session Musician.**   The session musician is the one responsible for playing background music in a studio while a recording artist is singing. The session musician may also be called a freelance musician, a backup musician, a session player, or studio musician. Session musicians are used for all kinds of recordings, Broadway musicals, operas, rock and folk songs, and pop tunes.

Versatility is the most important ingredient for these professionals—the more instruments the musician has mastered, the greater number of styles he or she can offer, the more possibilities for musical assignments. Session musicians often are listed through contractors who call upon them when the need arises. Other possibilities exist through direct requests made by the artists themselves, the group members, or the management team.

The ability to sight-read is important for all musicians but it is particularly crucial for session musicians. Rehearsal time is usually very limited and costs make it too expensive to have to do retakes.

**Section Leader—Section Member.**   Section members are the individuals who play instruments in an orchestra. They must be talented at playing their instrument of choice and able to learn the music on their own. Rehearsals are strictly designed for putting all of the instruments and individuals together, and for establishing cues such as phrasing and correct breathing. It is expected that all musicians practice sufficiently on their own before rehearsals.

**Concertmaster/Concertmistress.**  Those chosen to be concertmasters or concertmistresses have the important responsibility of leading the string sections of the orchestras during both rehearsals and concerts. In addition, these individuals are responsible for tuning the rest of the orchestra. This is the "music" you hear for about 15–20 seconds before the musicians begin to play their first piece.

Concertmasters and concertmistresses answer directly to the conductor and must possess leadership abilities and be very knowledgeable of both the music and all the instruments.

**Floor Show Band Member.**  Musicians who belong to bands that perform floor shows appear in hotels, nightclubs, cruise ships, bars, concert arenas, and cafes. Usually the bands do two shows per night with a particular number of sets in each show. Additionally, they may be required to play one or two dance sets during the course of the engagement. The audience is seated during the shows and gets up to dance during the dance sets. Shows may include costuming, dialogue, singing, jokes, skits, unusual sound effects, and anything else the band decides to include. Floor show bands may be contracted to appear in one place for one night or several weeks at a time. As expected, a lot of traveling is involved for those who take up this career.

**Choir Director/Church or Temple Musician.**  Choir directors are responsible for recruiting and directing choirs and planning the music programs. They are often given the job of auditioning potential members of the choir, setting up rehearsal schedules, overseeing and directing them, and choosing the music. They may be in charge of the church's or temple's music library or may designate another individual to do so. Working closely with the minister or other religious leader of the congregation, choir directors plan all concerts, programs, and other musical events.

In addition, choir directors develop and maintain the music budgets for their religious institutions. In some cases, choral directors are expected to maintain office hours each week. During those times, individuals may write music, handle administrative chores, or work with small groups of singers and/or the organist.

Usually a bachelor's degree in church music is required; often a master's degree is requested.

**Organist.**  Organists play their instruments at religious and special services like weddings and funerals. Recitals may also be given as part of the congregation's spiritual programming. Organists choose the music to be played or may work with the choir or music director to accomplish this task. Organists are also responsible for making sure organs are in proper working order and may also advise the congregation on other music-related issues. Sometimes the organist is also the choir director.

**Singer.** Singers use their voices as their instruments of choice. Using the techniques of melody, harmony, rhythm, and voice production, they interpret music and both instruct and entertain their audiences. They may sing character parts or perform in their own individual style.

Classical singers are identified by the ranges of their voices: Sopranos (highest range), contralto, tenor, baritone, and bass (lowest) range. These kinds of singers will typically perform in operas.

Singers of popular music may perform country and western, ethnic, reggae, folk, rock, or jazz as individuals or as part of a group. Often singers also possess the ability to play musical instruments and thus accompany themselves when performing (guitar or piano, for instance).

Religious singers include cantors, soloists, or choral members.

**Announcer/Disc Jockey.** Announcers play an important role in keeping listeners tuned in to a radio or television station. They are the ones who must read messages, commercials, and scripts in an entertaining, interesting, and/or enlightening way. They are also responsible for introducing station breaks, may interview guests, and sell commercial time to advertisers. Sometimes they are called disc jockeys, but actually disc jockeys are the announcers who oversee musical programming.

Disc jockeys must be very knowledgeable about music in general and all aspects of their specialties, specifically the music and the groups who play and/or sing that kind of music. Their programs may feature general music, rock, pop, country and western, or any specific musical period or style such as tunes from the 1950s or 1960s.

**Conductor and Choral Director.** The music conductor is the director for all of the performers in a musical presentation, whether it be singing or instrumental. Though there are many types of conductors—symphony, choral groups, dance bands, opera, marching bands, and ballet—in all cases the music conductor is the one who is in charge of interpreting the music.

Conductors audition and select musicians, choose the music to accommodate the talents and abilities of the musicians, and direct rehearsals and performances, applying conducting techniques to achieve desired musical effects like harmony, rhythm, tempo, and shading.

Orchestral conductors lead instrumental music groups, such as orchestras, dance bands, and various popular ensembles. Choral directors lead choirs and glee clubs, sometimes working with a band or orchestra conductor.

# POSSIBLE JOB TITLES

| | |
|---|---|
| Announcer | Musician |
| Cantor | Opera singer |
| Choir director | Organist |
| Choral director | Rock star |
| Church or temple musician | Recording group member |
| Concertmaster | Section leader |
| Conductor | Section member |
| Dance band member | Session musician |
| Disc jockey | Singer |
| Drummer | Star or member of musical |
| Folk guitarist | comedy production |
| Jingle singer | Violinist |

# POSSIBLE EMPLOYERS

Popular instrumentalists are distributed nationwide from small towns to large cities. Many consist of small groups that play at weddings, bar mitzvahs, church events, funerals, school or community concerts, dances, festivals, and other events. Accompanists play for theater productions or dance recitals. Combos, piano or organ soloists, and other musicians play at nightclubs, bars, or restaurants. Musicians may work in opera, musical comedy, and ballet productions or be a part of the Armed Forces. Well-known musicians and groups give their own concerts; appear "live" on radio and television; make recordings, movies, and music videos; or go on concert tours.

Many musicians work in cities in which there are fairly large populations and where entertainment and recording activities are concentrated, such as New York, Los Angeles, Nashville, San Francisco, Boston, Philadelphia, and Chicago.

Read the following trade magazines for possibilities:

*Billboard*
1515 Broadway
New York, NY 10036

*Cash Box*
51 East Eighth Street
Suite 155
New York, NY 10003

*Daily Variety*
5700 Wilshire Boulevard
Suite 120
Los Angeles, CA 90036

*Variety*
Cahners Publishing
475 Park Avenue South
New York, NY 10016

# RELATED OCCUPATIONS

| | | |
|---|---|---|
| composer | music sales | music librarian |
| songwriter | theatrical agent | music educator |
| piano tuner | music therapist | music critic |

# WORKING CONDITIONS

Musicians, singers, and conductors are often forced into work schedules which are long and erratic, depending on how heavy the rehearsal and presentation schedules are. Usually daily practices and/or rehearsals are required, particularly for new projects. Work weeks in excess of 40 hours are common. Travel is often a familiar part of a musician's or singer's life and a daytime, nighttime, weekend, and holiday work routine is entirely possible.

Musicians who are lucky enough to be hired for a full season (a "master agreement") work for up to 52 weeks. Those who must work for more than one employer are always on the lookout for additional "gigs," and many supplement their incomes by finding work in other related or nonrelated jobs.

Most instrumental musicians come into contact with a variety of other people, including their colleagues, agents, employers, sponsors, and audiences. They usually work indoors, although some may perform outdoors for parades, concerts, and dances. Certain performances create noise and vibration. In some taverns and restaurants, smoke and odors may be present and lighting and ventilation may be inadequate.

# TRAINING AND QUALIFICATIONS

Many people who become professional musicians begin studying their instrument of choice (whether it be voice, organ, harp, harpsichord, any string, woodwind, brass, or percussion) in childhood and continue the study via private or group lessons throughout elementary and high school. In addition, they usually garner valuable experience by playing in a school or community band or orchestra, or with a group of friends.

Singers usually start training when their voices mature. All musicians need extensive and prolonged training to acquire the necessary skills, knowledge, and ability to interpret music. Participation in school musicals, religious institutions, community events, state fairs, in a band, or in a choir often provides good early training and experience. Necessary formal training may be obtained through conservatory, college, or university study or personal study with a professional (or both).

Over 600 colleges, universities, and conservatories offer four-year programs that result in a bachelor's degree in music education. Usually both pop and classical music are studied. Course work will include classes in music theory, music composition, music interpretation, literature, conducting, drama, foreign languages, acting, and how to play a musical instrument. Other academic studies include course work in science, literature, philosophy, and the arts. Classroom instruction, discussion groups, reading assignments, and actual performances are included. A large number of performances are encouraged and expected and students are evaluated on their progress during their time at the college.

At the undergraduate level, a typical program for a violin major might consist of the following courses:

| | |
|---|---|
| Instrument | Piano and strings chamber music |
| Materials and literature | String quartet |
| Ear training | Introduction to literature |
| Piano class | Foreign language |
| Music history | Academic electives |
| Orchestra | |

Many schools offer advanced degrees in music. For instance, the Master of Music program at Webster University (Saint Louis, Geneva, Leiden, London, Vienna) includes the following course work for performance majors:

❑ Emphases
        Piano
        Voice
        Organ
        Classical guitar
        Orchestral instruments

❑ Required courses include:
        Applied Music, Major Instrument or Voice
        Analytical Technique I, II
        Seminar in Music Literature I, II
        Ensemble
        Electives
        Two public recitals
        Oral examination

❑ Suggested Electives:
        Eighteenth-Century Counterpoint
        The Art Song
        Operatic Literature
        Piano Literature I, II

Twentieth-Century Seminar (Topical)
Advanced Topics
Composition
Independent Study
Voice Pedagogy I, II
Piano Pedagogy I, II

## Advanced Studies in Music

Young persons who are considering careers in music need to have musical talent, improvisational skills, versatility, creative ability, the ability to sight-read, outstanding music memory, finger dexterity, ability to distinguish differences in pitch, determination, imagination, creativity, perseverance, ability to work with others, and poise and stage presence in order to face large audiences. Since quality performance requires constant study and practice, self-discipline is vital. Moreover, musicians who play concert and nightclub engagements must have physical stamina because frequent travel and night performances are required. They must also be prepared to face the anxiety of intermittent employment and rejections when auditioning for work.

For announcers and disc jockeys, additional education beyond secondary school, particularly course work in public speaking; writing; English; communications; music, radio, and television broadcasting; and videotape production is very advantageous. Desirable personal qualities include charisma, a pleasing voice, good timing, a good sense of humor, and expertise about the field of music. Experience as a production assistant or writer is also beneficial, as is securing a radio/telephone operator permit from the Federal Communications Commission (FCC).

Musical conductors must have at least a high school diploma and knowledge of: the arts; musical history, harmony, and theory; along with various languages (especially French, German, Latin, and Italian). Desirable qualities include charisma, a great ear for music, personal style, both business and musical savvy, knowledge of all instruments—particularly piano—advanced sight-reading skills, a sense of showmanship, the ability to lead, skills in performing in an appealing way, and the ability to use a baton to control timing, rhythm, and structure. Individuals become musical conductors after spending many years as musicians while, at the same time, studying to become conductors.

# *E*ARNINGS

Earnings in the world of music performing will depend heavily on a number of factors: experience, training, the specific instrument played, reputation, location, and whether or not you belong to a union. Bear in mind that salaries must cover expenses, travel, publicity costs, and agent or manager fees. Royalty figures average about ten to twelve percent—escalating all the way up to twenty-five percent if you are a top entertainer.

Musicians are covered by the American Federation of Musicians videotape agreement guaranteeing a minimum two-hour call with payment of $55.15 per hour. Varying pay scales exist for basic cable television and documentary films.

Here are some sample earnings:

---

### Symphony orchestra

Metropolitan: $35 to $85 per concert in addition to $25 to $50 per rehearsal

Regional: $400 to $700 per week (average 30-week year, may extend to 52 weeks)

Major: $1,000 to $1,400 per week ($50,000 to $60,000 per year), 48 to 52 working weeks per year

Soloist: $60,000 to $70,000 per year

Broadway musical: $600 to $1,000 per week for 20 working hours

Freelance musician: $40 per 2.5 hour rehearsal

Freelance (union) musician: $85 per performance

**Jazz musicians:** $100 to $300 per night

**Jazz groups:** $2,000 to $3,000 per week at a well-established nightclub

**Studio musicians:** $250 for a three-hour session, plus $50 for each additional thirty minutes

**Motion picture recording:** $200 to $260 per week depending on size of ensemble

**Sound or music editor:** $1,400 per week

---

Popular musicians may be paid for a single performance or for a number of engagements. The pay could range anywhere from $30 per performance to $300 per performance. Jazz musicians in popular clubs in New York City earn $100 to $300 per night while musicians in a Broadway musical orchestra could receive more than $600 a week for twenty hours of work. When available, studio recording pays well—more than $175 for a three-hour session.

Earnings for singers will vary considerably depending upon the location, their experience, and the magnitude of the event. The following provide examples of earnings:

### Television and Radio

Groups of three to eight:
>$478 on camera
>$288 off camera

Groups of nine or more:
>$417 on camera
>$250 off camera

(Source: SAG contract, 1994–1995. Payment regulated by AFTRA/SAG)

### Radio Dealer commercials for a six-month period

(Dealer commercials are made for a designated manufacturer for delivery to and use by its local dealers. Dealer contracts station time and is limited to use as a wild spot or local program commercial.)

Actor, Announcer: $606.20

Solo or Duo: $480.85

Groups:
>Three to five—$313.50
>Six to eight—$250.85
>Nine or more—$156.75

Sound Effects:
>Performer—$158.55

(Source: AFTRA)

### Opera

Singer in a leading role: $650 minimum per week

Solo bits: $541 per week (plus diem for a maximum of six weeks)

Well-known singer: $2,000 to $4,000 at small houses

Choral members: $950 to $1,100 per week at the Metropolitan Opera in New York

Star performers: $12,000 per performance at the Metropolitan Opera in New York

(Source: most salaries set by the American Guild of Musical Artists (AGMA))

Though earnings for announcers and disc jockeys will vary according to the experience, area of the country, and size of the market, salaries tend to be higher in television stations. Average salaries for announcers in a small station would be $22,000 per year to start. A larger station would probably offer about $45,000 per year.

Conductors often negotiate on a one-to-one basis with individual orchestras to determine a salary. The size of the orchestra and the location will be factors in determining figures. However, sample figures follow:

Part-time choir directors: $3,500 to $25,000 per year (church)
Full-time choir directors: $15,000 to $40,000 per year (church)
Dance band: $300 to $1,200 per week
Full-time opera conductor (established): $100,000
Regional conductor: $25,000 to $40,000
International conductor: $500,000 per year

Since they may not work steadily for one employer, some performers may not qualify for unemployment compensation, and few have either sick leave or vacations with pay. For these reasons, many musicians give private lessons or take jobs unrelated to music in order to supplement their earnings as performers.

Many musicians belong to a local chapter of the American Federation of Musicians (AFM). Professional singers usually belong to a branch of the Associated Actors and Artists of America (AAAA).

## CAREER OUTLOOK

Competition for musician jobs is keen, and talent alone is no guarantee of success. The glamour and potential high earnings in this occupation attract many talented individuals.

The *Occupational Outlook Handbook* published by the U.S. Department of Labor reports that overall employment of musicians is expected to grow faster than the average for all occupations through the year 2005. Almost all new wage and salary jobs for musicians will arise in religious organizations and bands, orchestras, and other entertainment groups. A decline in employment is projected for salaried musicians in restaurants and bars, although they comprise a very small proportion of the total number of musicians who are salaried.

Competition is always great for announcers/disc jockeys. They must often work on a freelance basis rather than a regular, yearly, salaried basis. The growth in the areas of cable television and of licensing of new radio and television stations indicates an increase in the number of jobs that will be available through the year 2005.

The outlook for musical conductors is not especially positive. Competition is always fierce for the limited jobs that exist.

## STRATEGY FOR FINDING THE JOBS

### The Job Search

Getting ready for a job search is like getting ready to do battle: You must arm yourself with all the best weapons available to you and plan the best possible plan of attack. The best weapons available to you include a well-designed resume, a well-conceived cover letter, a well-selected portfolio, and an audition tape in video or audio.

## The Resume

A resume should include significant information that would make an employer want to hire you above all others. Standing as a summary of your experience, skills and abilities, strengths, accomplishments, and education, its importance cannot be underestimated.

Experts agree that the best approach is to keep it focused and as brief as possible. Complete sentences are not necessary; phrases are acceptable. Keep to a maximum of two pages—one is even better. Don't list everything you ever did in your life; highlight important skills and accomplishments.

One type of resume, the *chronological resume*, includes the following elements:

**1. Heading.** Provide a heading at the top of the page that includes your name, home address, e-mail, and phone number(s). Invest in an answering machine or answering service if you don't already have one.

**2. Work Experience.** This will be the main part of your resume, where your prospective employers will focus to determine whether or not you have the right qualifications for the job. So here is where you must show your expertise by emphasizing your accomplishments. Use action verbs. Passive words don't have the same impact. Work experience is usually listed in reverse chronological order, beginning with your most recent position and working back. Entries should be complete, listing the job title, dates of employment, employer, and location.

**3. Education.** Next to work experience, education is most important. Include all of the schools you've attended, the degrees you've earned, your field of concentration, and relevant extracurricular activities (student choral director, for example).

**4. Professional Associations.**

**5. Awards and Honors.**

**6. Special Skills.**

**7. References.**

## The Cover Letter

A cover letter is a document that sells the recipient on reading the resume. It should be directed to a specific person whose name and spelling you have verified. Cover letters should be tailored to each specific company or job opening. Don't use a form letter here, although some of the information, including the job you are seeking and some elements of your professional background, may be the same.

Cover letters should consist of the following elements:

**1. A Salutation.** This is to the person who can hire you.

**2. The Opening.** Start with something that catches the attention of the reader. Be creative! Introduce yourself and specify the job for which you want to be considered. If you have a referral name, by all means mention it, and if you are responding to an ad, state that. If possible, show your researching skills by pointing out something new or positive you know about this employment possibility.

**3. The Body.** This provides a brief summary of your qualifications for the job and refers to the resume, which will reinforce your selling campaign to win an interview or audition.

**4. The Closing.** Here you should request an interview and state your intention to follow up with a call, preferably on a specific date. Use the standard "Sincerely yours" and type your name, leaving room for you to sign in between. It's not a bad idea to put your address and phone number under your name in the event the letter gets separated from the resume.

## Avenues to Jobs

Those who study music at educational institutions may find their first jobs by going through their school placement offices. Working closely with these human resource professionals can provide you with a wealth of worthwhile advice. For example, since orchestra musicians usually audition for positions after completing their formal training, school employment services may provide you with a list of possible locations.

Finding positions through want ads or ads published in trade journals is still a popular form of securing jobs. Also, professional organizations and associations may offer you direct employment possibilities or provide you with agencies, companies, or other employers or contacts that may eventually evolve into positions. Consider joining one that caters to your own musical specialty or to the field of music in general.

It is important to know that, no matter what the field, the majority of people find their jobs through networking. This means that you must make a concerted effort to let people know what your expertise is and that you are available. Talk to friends and acquaintances; go to club meetings and association workshops. Volunteer to help with an event. Converse with people you deal with in everyday life: cleaners, bank tellers, personal accountants, anyone you can think of. Of course, you may not hear about an opening directly, but one person may give you the name of another contact that *will* eventually lead to a job. In the music business, it is wise to get to know as many people as possible, not only to make contacts that will lead to jobs, but in order to make contacts that may lead to internships, volunteer, or part-time work.

Send a resume and cover letter to everyone you know who has any link to the music business. Let people know if you have a videocassette or audiotape of you performing. If they want to hear it, they'll get back in touch. Don't send these things out if they are not requested. Keep track of the responses and follow up with people you don't hear from.

Individual musicians often join together with others to form local bands. Once formed, you can advertise by placing ads, putting up notices, and spread the message by word of mouth. After building a reputation, you may be able to obtain work through a booking agent or be qualified to become part of larger, more established groups.

After having some performing under your belt, you might visit recording studios and talk to anyone you can. Tell them about yourself, your experience, your musical specialties. Make sure you leave your business card (or a sheet with the information listed) with your instrument written on it. In fact, always carry cards with you and pass them out whenever you possibly can. You may need to have a demo tape made to leave with possible employers. Demos are recordings of your work (singing or instrumental) that display your talents at their very best!

## PROFESSIONAL ASSOCIATIONS

There are literally hundreds of professional associations that provide benefits to members. Here are some of them:

**American Choral Directors Association (ACDA)**
PO Box 6310
Lawton, OK 73506

**American Federation of Musicians (AFM)**
1501 Broadway, Suite 600
New York, NY 10036

**American Federation of Television and Radio Artists (AFTRA)**
260 Madison Avenue
New York, NY 10016

**American Guild of Musical Artists (AGMA)**
1727 Broadway
New York, NY 10019

**American Guild of Organists (AGO)**
475 Riverside Drive, Suite 1260
New York, NY 10115

**American Guild of Music (AGM)**
5354 Washington Street, Box 3
Downers Grove, IL 60515

**American Music Conference (AMC)**
5140 Avenida Encinas
Carlsbad, CA 92008

**American Musicological Society**
University of Pennsylvania
201 South 34th Street
Philadelphia, PA 19104

**American Symphony Orchestra League (ASOL)**
777 Fourteenth Street, N.W., Suite 500
Washington, DC 20005

**Academy of Country Music (ACM)**
500 Sunnyside Boulevard
Woodbury, NY 11797

**Association of Canadian Orchestras**
56 The Esplanade, Suite 311
Toronto, Canada M5E 1A7

**Black Music Association (BMA)**
1775 Broadway
New York, NY 10019

**Broadcast Music, Inc. (BMI)**
320 West 57th Street
New York, NY 10019

**Chamber Music America**
545 Eighth Avenue
New York, NY 10018

**Chorus America**
Association of Professional Vocal Ensembles
2111 Sansom Street
Philadelphia, PA 19103

**College Music Society**
202 West Spruce
Missoula, MT 59802

**Concert Artists Guild (CAG)**
850 Seventh Avenue, Room 1003
New York, NY 10019

**Country Music Association (CMA)**
One Music Circle South
P.O. Box 22299
Nashville, TN 37203

**Gospel Music Association (GMA)**
P.O. Box 23201
Nashville, TN 37202

**International Conference of Symphony and Opera Musicians (ICSOM)**
6607 Waterman
St. Louis, MO 63130

**Metropolitan Opera Association (MOA)**
Lincoln Center
New York, NY 10023

**National Academy of Popular Music (NAPM)**
885 Second Avenue
New York, NY 10017

**National Academy of Recording Arts and Sciences (NARAS)**
303 N. Glen Oaks Boulevard, Suite 140
Burbank, CA 91502

**National Association of Music Theaters**
John F. Kennedy Center
Washington, DC 20566

**National Association of Schools of Music**
11250 Roger Bacon Drive, Suite 21
Reston, VA 22091

**National Orchestral Association (NOA)**
474 Riverside Drive, Room 455
New York, NY 10115

**National Symphony Orchestra Association (NSOA)**
JFK Center for the Performing Arts
Washington, DC 20566

**Opera America**
777 14th Street, N.W., Suite 520
Washington, DC 20005

**Society of Professional Audio Recording Studios**
4300 Tenth Avenue North, No. 2
Lake Worth, FL 33461

**Screen Actors Guild (SAG)**
7065 Hollywood Boulevard
Hollywood, CA 90028

**Touring Entertainment Industry Association (TEIA)**
1203 Lake Street
Fort Worth, TX 76102

**Women in Music**
Radio City Station
P.O. Box 441
New York, NY 10101

---

### MEET MARK MAREK

Mark Marek is a singer and the owner of Private Stock Variety Dance Band of Lenexa, Kansas. His background includes two years of college with course work focusing on music theory, audio and engineering, and the fundamentals of music and business.

"I started playing the drums in junior high school and then learned how to play the six-string guitar," says Mark. "By the time I was sixteen, my brother had his own band so I started playing and learning about bands from him. Fourteen years ago, I started my own band.

"We are primarily a country club/high dollar type band," explains Mark. "We play mostly at weddings, country clubs, and other formal occasions. The band's working hours are usually 6:30 P.M. until 1:00 A.M., mostly on Fridays and Saturdays. Most gigs usually last three to four hours and we have to arrive at a gig at least an hour and a half before the start time. We generally do one-hour sets, with a twenty-minute break every hour or so. In addition to setting up for the gig, we also have to break down the equipment. Because we've been together for so long, we don't need to rehearse much, perhaps every three to four months.

"I love seeing the reaction of the audience," says Mark. "It's fun to know and see that they are having a good time. That's the thrill I get

continued

continued

out of it. What I least like is the inconsistency in bookings. Each month the number of gigs changes, which affects the cash flow. The peak periods for the band are December and May/June.

"During the week, I mostly book gigs, spend time on the phone getting the specifics for each gig, and contact the five band members about our schedule. I also handle all of the contracts for each gig. Aside from the band, I also give private guitar lessons and book gigs for other bands.

"To approach success in the music industry you need to have good people skills, a general sense of business, a real enjoyment for what you do, a recognition of what your niche is in the music world, patience, good customer relations skills, expert technical skills, and a knowledge of audio and video.

"Having a band is a business, not an ego trip," says Mark. "You really need to have a basic knowledge of business and marketing. You can be the best musician, but you have to know how to sell yourself in order to be successful. It's a tough way to make a living—that's why you have to really have a passion for the business."

## MEET ED GOEKE

Ed Goeke is the Music Director of Christ Episcopal Church in Overland Park, Kansas. He has a BA/MA in Music Education from the University of Iowa and a MA from the University of Kansas in Lawrence, Kansas, where he is a Ph.D. candidate in Music Education.

"I studied voice, piano, and French horn from the time I was in junior high school," he says. "Both of my parents are music educators, so it was a natural thing for me to enter a career in music. Music has affected my whole life. It is my life. I can't imagine not having musical outlets. I will probably never leave music. What I find most gratifying is performing well, knowing that people are grateful for a job well done.

"Sunday is the culmination of the work I do all week. The day starts around 8:00 A.M. with warm-up for the first service, which is at 8:45 A.M. This is an ensemble of 8 to 10 people. When this service is over, then rehearsal starts (9:30 or so) for the 10:45 service. This is a choir of 24 people with an organist. The service is over around noon. There is a break for lunch, then around 2:30 rehearsal starts for the 5:30 service. We organize and plan for this week's service and some for next week's selection. The day usually ends around 7:00 P.M.

continued

continued

"It's very casual here in terms of dress and chain of command. There is lots of time spent in rehearsal and planning for worship services. The busiest time is the whole month of December due to the number of liturgies and the importance of the spiritual services.

"I took this job because it enables me to use my classical background and work in a traditional setting, but at the same time lead others in contemporary music. I can work with a variety of musicians. It's great working with this fine group of people. I like best working with a mission in mind—having a goal of bringing people closer to God through worship by providing windows of opportunity through excellent music. The music allows people to participate more actively by providing a means that inspires/moves people more deeply to developing a closer relationship with God. What I like least is reproducing music and having to stay on top of all of the paperwork.

"Church jobs are changing dramatically; the best way to be equipped is to get very good at one thing. If you want to be a music director of a church full time, then it is important to have excellent keyboarding skills. I'd recommend gaining skills in arranging and improvisational skills, and exposure to a wide variety of music. It is important to be able to work well with people. This can be accomplished by acquiring experience of performing in church choirs.

"It's important that you are a people person, that you are a team builder/consensus builder, that you are sensitive to people's needs, that you have a thorough knowledge of what makes music good, have a background in performance, keyboard skills, good knowledge of literature for choirs, a background in liturgy, the ability to take available resources and arrange on the spot, good improvisational skills, the ability to communicate effectively, and good organizational skills."

# CHAPTER ELEVEN

# PATH 2: BEHIND THE SCENES

*Let me die to the sounds of delicious music.*

## Last words of Mirabeau

W hen you were younger and taking part in performances, did you long to be the center of attention with all eyes focused on you or did you prefer the idea of staying in the background helping with props, lighting, or sound? When you went to a performance, did you ever think about what was going on behind the scenes? Did you ever consider how many people had a role in making sure that everything went according to plan?

Most people don't have any idea about what goes on behind the scenes and how many professionals perform a variety of tasks in order to make a performance successful and as entertaining as possible.

## DEFINITION OF THE CAREER PATH

Team spirit is of the utmost importance for the professionals who work together behind the scenes to create performances everyone can be proud of. Those who work behind the scenes include stage managers, boom operators, sound/production mixers, sound and lighting technicians, music video producers, and record producers.

# CAREER CHOICES: BEHIND THE SCENES

## Stage Manager

Stage managers are in charge of everything involved in onstage performances whether they are held at clubs, concert halls, state fairs, theaters, or any other arena. All aspects of a performance come under the stage manager's domain— curtain changes, lighting, sound—anything and everything that could have an effect upon the success of the performance. He or she is thus in charge of all technicians, assistants, and helpers—the entire staff.

Sometimes, important stars travel with their own lighting and sound technicians' crews. As a result, the stars feel they can relax in the fact that their crews are very familiar with what needs to be done and there will be no unpleasant "surprises" before, during, or after performances.

## Sound Technician/ Sound Engineer

Sound technicians are important members of the behind-the-scenes staff. They answer to the tour coordinator and usually arrive at the location of the performance in advance of the performers. Along with the rest of the crew, sound technicians unload and set up the equipment and the instruments. All of the equipment must be positioned so that the instruments will sound their best and vocals, if part of the performance, will blend in a pleasing manner.

Once things are set up, the vocalists and musicians arrive and the sound technicians prepare for a very important event—the sound check. This is accomplished by having each person sing or play his or her instrument, while technicians judge whether or not the sound is coming through properly. Obviously, any changes that need to be made will be taken care of before the show begins.

While the show is in progress, sound technicians are in charge of the sound board, usually situated in front of the stage. From here they can adjust the volumes of voices and instruments.

After the show, sound technicians usually pack up the sound equipment. In some cases they may be responsible for checking all of the equipment to see what is not working properly or is in need of repair. The sound technicians may also be capable of actually taking care of the problem.

## Boom Operator

The boom is a large overhead microphone that hangs over the set. The boom operator makes sure that the boom is properly following the performers.

## Sound/Production Mixer

The sound/production mixer is in charge of the overall sound quality and the volume of the sound. Required when there is more than one microphone on the set, sound/production mixers make sure that sound is picked up and blended in a harmonious way.

## Music Video Producer

Music video producers are in charge of everything relating to the making of music videos. This includes all of the visual effects and interpretations of the songs vocal artists are endeavoring to promote. Producers oversee the entire production team including film editor, choreographer, photography director, and the rest of the team.

Music video producers must be superb problem solvers, have good visual and listening proficiencies, the ability to work well with others, a good business sense, a sufficient understanding of the business, and good contacts in the industry.

## Record Producer

There are many people who are part of the process of record production. Perhaps most important is the record producer. Record producers have the important responsibilities of handling all payroll tasks, supervising the recording sessions, helping to decide what songs will be recorded, and actually producing the records for the artists. Other responsibilities include finding a suitable recording studio, arranging the recording time, choosing an engineer, picking an arranger, and getting in touch with someone who can find the background musicians and vocalists needed. Record producers will also act as the heads of the operations, making sure everyone meets their responsibilities. While actually recording, the producer works hand in hand with the engineer to create the exact sound desired.

## Recording Engineer

The recording engineer operates the sound board and other electrical equipment when recordings are made.

## Recordist

This technician operates the tape machine and makes sure that everything is recorded properly.

## Rerecording Mixer

Rerecording mixers complete soundtracks by adding background music, additional dialogue, or sound effects.

# Possible Job Titles

| | |
|---|---|
| Audio technician | Recordist |
| Boom operator | Rerecording mixer |
| General director | Resident sound technician |
| Music video producer | Sound engineer |
| Program director | Sound technician |
| Recording engineer | Sound/production mixer |
| Recording studio set-up worker | Stage manager |

# Possible Employers

Behind-the-scenes technicians may find employment with a local or well-known regional band. The best strategy is to start small and try to work your way to larger and more well-known bands. Major tours usually traverse Los Angeles, New York City, and Nashville although they may be found in almost any substantially sized city in the United States.

# Related Occupations

| | |
|---|---|
| Assistant stage manager | Recording assistant |
| Audio technician | Recording engineer |
| Engineer | Recording studio clerk |
| Engineer–producer | Roadie |
| Grip | Sound engineer |
| Lighting technician | Stagehand |

# Working Conditions

Traveling all the time can present a lifestyle with a number of challenges. Long periods on the road living out of suitcases and away from family and friends can be a very difficult existence. Since performances may be held daytime, evening, or weekend hours, working times may be virtually at any time of the day or night.

# TRAINING AND QUALIFICATIONS

Though a formal education is not required for those who work behind the scenes, it can provide you with a concrete background of information and contacts. A number of individuals interested in this field acquire basic knowledge and experience by "shadowing" other individuals who are performing this kind of work.

Working as a volunteer in community, church, or school productions offers valuable experience that will help to elevate your marketability in the music business.

It's important for behind-the-scenes personnel to be able to work well with all kinds of people because they serve as a link in the chain that provides the totality of music performances. Other desirable characteristics include reliability; responsibility; a good ear for music; sufficient expertise in the areas of musical and technical knowledge; proficiency with the sound board, sound equipment, and electronics; and a love of music.

# EARNINGS

Sound technicians working for a local band that is just getting started may earn only minimum wage or even less. As an average, however, sound technicians earn from about $15,000 to about $45,000 or more each year. Higher salaries will go to sound technicians who accompany better-known groups on the road. (It is also important to realize that a freelance sound technician may well not work every week.)

Earnings and benefits vary widely depending on the location, medium, and experience of the individual. The following represent typical averages:

Broadcast technicians (radio): $440 per week
Broadcast technician (television): $500 per week
Sound crew members: $500 to $600 per week for eight performances in New York
Beginning sound mixers: $700 to $800 per week
Mixers with experience: $1,400 per week
Sound recordist: $840 per week
Stage manager: $12,000 to $40,000 and up annually
Music video producer
    Entry-level trainee: $16,000 to $18,000

continued

> continued
>
> Experienced music video producer: $35,000 to $40,000
> Producer with his or her own company: $100,000 to $300,000

Staff record producers may be entitled to a salary plus royalties on the numbers of records produced. This may amount to $18,000 to $45,000 per year and up. Those who freelance will probably be paid a fee by the artist or the record label, again in addition to royalties on works produced. Terms will vary considerably depending on who you are and what your established reputation is. It is possible for a record producer to earn in excess of $250,000 per year.

## CAREER OUTLOOK

Competition is very stiff for behind-the-scenes professionals. Technicians may often be hired as "grips" (individuals who move equipment such as cameras, etc.) first and work their way up. The emergence of cable television has produced a need for more technicians.

There are possibilities for individuals to become record producers, but only after they have paid their dues and built their knowledge and reputations. Once this happens, producers can go to other labels that are more prestigious and pay higher salaries.

## STRATEGY FOR FINDING THE JOBS

The classified section of the newspaper may offer opportunities. It's also wise to check trade journals and association bulletins for possible employment openings or job leads. You might also go directly to theaters, concert halls, clubs, and similar places and speak to the manager. Be sure to bring along a resume that contains a list of your accomplishments and experience. Hanging around clubs and other places where there is live entertainment will enhance your body of knowledge and perhaps provide contacts that will materialize into jobs now or later.

Offering your services as a roadie might provide experience and knowledge and also possibly land you a job in the future.

If you possibly can, offer your services for free for a short period of time and learn everything there is to know about working behind the scenes or for a recording studio. Check into seminars, workshops, associations, and internship programs that may prove worthwhile for information and contacts.

To gain entry as a record producer, first get your foot in the door and work your way up—floor manager, engineer, receptionist, whatever it takes. Then watch how producers do their jobs. It's always a good idea to work hard to get an internship at a recording studio. This is always a good way for you to build solid contacts and solid experience and expertise in your chosen field. New York, Los Angeles, or Nashville offer the best possibilities.

Examples include:

**Arista Records**
6 West 57th Street
New York, NY 10019
Contact: Human Resources

**Cleopatra Records**
P.O Box 1394
Hollywood, CA 90078

**SONY Music and Entertainment, Inc.**
550 Madison Avenue, 2nd Floor
New York, NY 10022-3211
Contact: Recruitment Department

# PROFESSIONAL ASSOCIATIONS

Resident sound technicians may choose to belong to the International Alliance of Theatrical Stage Employees (IATSE), a bargaining union for professionals employed in the theater.

**Acoustical Society of America (ASA)**
500 Sunnyside Boulevard
Woodbury, NY 11797

**Electronic Industry Association (EIA)**
2001 Pennsylvania Avenue NW
Washington, DC 20006

**International Alliance of Theatrical Stage Employees (IATSE)**
Local 33 IATSE
1720 West Magnolia Boulevard
Burbank, CA 91506

**International Association of Auditorium Managers (IAAM)**
4425 West Airport Freeway
Irving, TX 75062

**International Brotherhood of Electrical Workers (IBEW)**
1125 Fifteenth Street NW
Washington, DC 20005

**National Association of Broadcast Employees and Technicians (NABET)**
7101 Wisconsin Avenue, Suite 800
Bethesda, MD 20814

**Society of Professional Audio Recording Studios (SPARS)**
4300 Tenth Avenue North
Lake Worth, FL 33461

---

### MEET ROSS NORTON

Ross Norton's educational background includes an Associate's Degree in Instructional Technology from the University of Phoenix. Work experience includes positions as production/stage manager, backline/guitar technician, and lighting systems technician in Nashville, Tennessee.

"I wanted to be close to the music," says Ross. "As a teenager, I was a regular concertgoer and found myself always wanting more. I felt that making a living working around something that gave me so much pleasure was the best of both worlds.

"Over the years I have acquired quite a few different job descriptions as the need arose," Ross explains. "I originally started out with a lighting company that leased out lights and crews to go with them to different bands touring the circuit of major venues. I now do stage managing and production and was recently the site coordinator for Country Fest '96 in Atlanta.

"Lighting presents a kind of work that is definitely the most brutal. The gear is awkward and heavy. The work hours are long, thankless, and dirty, and the pay for a beginner is next to nothing. Lights are always the first in and the last out and you will earn every nickel of spare time that you can find. There is no glamour and never has been to this kind of lifestyle. Lighting technicians are definitely the hardest working and most durable of all touring personnel.

"It does, however, provide you with a foot in the door to an otherwise closed room. It will allow you to get a glimpse of how things work at a show, to help you decide if you want to work in this industry or not.

"It won't seem like it at first, but all shows are basically run the same. A typical day starts weeks in advance with calls from the band's production manager to the local promoter who is sponsoring the show. This is

continued

continued

called advance work, and how well it's done can definitely affect your day. This is where the number of stagehands (local boys and girls brought in to help the road crew) is decided and all the stage and rigging requirements are hashed out so there will be as few surprises as possible when the trucks arrive. Each lighting and sound configuration is different with each band. Every single cable, chain, and bulb is brought in by the band unless otherwise ordered (and when we leave, nothing is left but dust and an empty stage).

"The trucks usually arrive around eight or nine in the morning and you are paying for the local crew whether you use them or not so you had best be quick. The riggers will climb up into the ceiling of the venue and begin hanging points. These are motors that hoist up the lights and sound above the stage. The lighting crew will begin assembling the lighting rig on the stage. A good stage manager will already have checked out the condition of the stage to make sure that it is level, big enough (as per your advance work), and has no weak spots that could cave as gear is added to it. While the lights are being assembled on stage, the sound PA is being unloaded and pushed (as all the gear is) out to the floor in front of the stage. This push could be a matter of feet or, in some cases, a hundred yards through an alley and up to a window on the second floor. It just depends on the building and what it has available.

"There are three distinct and different crews that make up a tour: the lighting crew, sound crew, and the band's personal band crew who set up and take care of their band gear, guitars, etc. These "band aides," as they are sometimes called, also include the production manager, stage manager, and overall tour manager who usually travels with the band and deals with all of their needs.

"The call for band crew is usually around noon or one o'clock. They are the last in and the first out (which can definitely cause tension). After all, the rest of the crew has been hard at work for quite a while. Once the band gear is placed and checked, lights focused, and sound gear tested, we have what is known as a sound check. This usually happens around three in the afternoon and can run anywhere from ten minutes to three hours. Sometimes the band crew (usually musicians themselves) will play the gear for this. If not, this can make for an ugly sound check for those forced to listen. By five in the evening the lights are done, providing they all worked. This is not to be held against the light crew. The gear is delicate, and being trucked and handled on a daily basis takes its toll on even the toughest of gear. The PA is up and now if you think you can take a break—

continued

continued

you're wrong. The opening act has yet to set up and all of their gear has to be miked, tested, and a sound check conducted. Band gear, stage monitors, and other equipment will all have to be struck from the stage or moved to accommodate the new gear so that there is room for the act. This is usually finished and wrapped up around seven or so in the evening. Doors to the house are now open and any work you have to do at this point is done with the crowd present. Fun, huh?

"Depending on your job, you may or may not have to work during the show," says Ross. "The band crew will be all over the stage changing guitars as well as at least one senior light technician. Anything that breaks during the show, you have to fix it during the show. This is the most stressful on the band crew because though you might be able to do the show with a few less lights, it's pretty hard to pull off if the lead guitar rig goes down. A couple of screwups by the band crew during a show usually gets you an early plane ticket home. Any production manager worth his salt has got a long list of band gear technicians who are always ready to replace you for less money than what you are making.

"Once the show is over, you are moving quickly. You could have as much as two to ten tractor trailers full of gear hanging from the roof or on the stage and it all has to come down and be loaded. This is the hardest part of the day because it is a fast and furious pace and road crews take exceptional pride in their load out times. Usually by two in the morning the gear is back on the trucks and the crew bus is waiting. Now it is on to the next city because the next show loads in at eight in the morning. Enjoy.

"Throughout the entire day, there is an unseen dance going on between stagehands, lighting and sound crew, as well as the band crew and promoter representatives. Everyone knows the dance and performs it without even thinking, until a new face shows up that hasn't danced before. One inexperienced person can cause more damage and bodily harm than any other single factor on the road. They trip over cables and sometimes guitars. They put things where they don't belong, don't know who to ask for help, and are usually in the way. If you're new on the road, keep a low profile (that means that you stay low and let us make the profile) and do **exactly** what you are told. As the years go by, you will learn the dance and hopefully won't have gotten anybody killed in the process. You will also learn who not to talk to during the day. Most road people have been doing this sort of thing for years and know everyone at the halls you will be playing. They have earned a reputation

continued

continued

(some good and some bad) but no one wants to hear from the new kid. The day is too short and the hours too long. Ask a million questions of your immediate supervisor, but that is about the length of it in the beginning. Watch and learn. Nothing is done without a reason, no matter how trivial it may seem. There just isn't time for anything else.

"We get an incredible feeling from seeing and hearing a crowd jump on its feet and scream. It's our job satisfaction to know that without us none of it would have been possible. The best way to make the impossible happen with us is to tell us that it can't be done. Not only will we show you that it can, but it can be done better than you had hoped. We don't get our names in lights and don't care. There is no limousine waiting for us. We don't want to be stars or hang out with stars. We just do our job and go home to the family. We don't broadcast to people what we do for a living because we don't want to answer the same dumb question every place we go. What's it like? What's it like? What's it like? The answer is—we simply love what we do."

# CHAPTER TWELVE

# PATH 3: THE BUSINESS OF MUSIC

*Music, the greatest good that mortals know,
And all of heaven we have below.*

## Joseph Addison, "Song for St. Cecilia's Day"

I n the world at large, the art of negotiation by a third party has been in existence ever since individuals began communicating with one another. This job of "facilitator" was historically given to the individual who, for a fee, would arrange an audience with important officials (or royalty) or set up a meeting for those seeking a face-to-face encounter. Today, in the world of entertainment, that job is often handled by individuals called personal managers, business managers, booking agents, or artists' agents who act as representatives and negotiators for their clients.

## DEFINITION OF THE CAREER PATH

Are you knowledgeable about the world of music but not comfortable actually performing? Do you have a desire to handle the business end of things? Can you speak persuasively? Are you good with figures? Perhaps you might be interested in becoming an artist's representative, personal manager, or booking agent.

# CAREER CHOICES: THE BUSINESS OF MUSIC

## Artist's Representative or Personal/Business Manager

Personal managers, also called artists' representatives, are responsible for representing artists. Their specific responsibilities may vary but, in many cases, they are in charge of all aspects of a music performer's career, promoting their client's interests whenever and wherever possible. This includes business decisions and may also include all or some creative decisions.

Agents may represent many artists at one time. Sometimes agents specialize and only represent one type of performer or even one type of music—such as rock music. They may work for a large or small agency or be self-employed.

Much of an agent's time is spent on the phone, fax, or e-mail—discussing prospects, arranging meetings, making networking connections, and keeping in touch with what is going on in the industry.

One of the most important jobs for agents is to negotiate contracts. Other duties include seeing to and improving costuming, choreography, backup musicians, and tunes; arranging publicity; and providing guidance for their client performers. If the entertainer is well established, the manager may be in charge of support personnel including publicists or public relations firms, road personnel, security people, accountants, producers, musicians, and merchandisers. Successful managers are always in constant communication with the act's booking agent or agency.

Business managers concentrate on the financial affairs of the singers, musicians, and other entertainers whom they represent. They are often the ones who negotiate with agents or representatives for contracts and appearances. They may also negotiate with television producers, record companies, and motion picture studios and sometimes seek large endorsements of concert tours. They are in charge of all fiscal disbursements, making sure the bills are in order and that the payroll for all employees in the act (including road personnel, musicians, vocalists, publicists, public relations firms, lawyers, etc.) is dispensed properly. Business managers may even possibly be in charge of the artist's personal bills.

## Booking Agents

Booking agents are also called theatrical agents, booking managers, booking representatives, agents, or bookers. These professionals are in charge of arranging engagements for both solo musical artists and/or groups for movies, television programming, concerts, and live performances. They usually represent a number of clients at a time. Sometimes they are chosen to act as talent buyers for concert halls or clubs or may open their own talent agency.

# Possible Job Titles

There are a number of possible titles with overlapping responsibilities; some of them alternate names for the same job:

| | |
|---|---|
| Agent | Booking representative |
| Artist's representative | Business manager |
| Booker | Personal manager |
| Booking agent | Talent agent |
| Booking manager | Theatrical agent |

# Possible Employers

Any performer is a possible employer for an agent or business or personal manager. Cities like New York, Los Angeles, and Chicago, with large entertainment opportunities, will present more possibilities for employment. The following represent companies available to those who are established and have experience:

**Columbia Artists Management**
165 West 57th Street
New York, NY 10019
Contact: Human Resources

**International Creative Management**
40 West 57th Street
New York, NY 10019
Contact: Director of Personnel

**International Management Group**
One Erieview Plaza, Suite 1300
Cleveland, OH 44114
Contact: Director of Human Resources

# Related Occupations

Some of the same skills required for artist's representatives are necessary for the following occupations:

| | |
|---|---|
| Accountant | Personnel manager |
| Business manager | Press secretary |
| Consultant | Real estate agent |
| Contract negotiator | Road manager |
| Insurance broker | Sales professional |
| Lawyer | Statistician |
| Manufacturers representative | Tour coordinator |
| Music editor | Travel agent |
| Music executive | Union negotiator |

## WORKING CONDITIONS

This is not a forty-hour-week career. Weekend and evening work is to be expected, and the pace is a busy one. The job may require travel, perhaps extensive, exploring new sources for clients and meeting with prospective employers.

## TRAINING AND QUALIFICATIONS

Though there are no specific educational requirements for many of these careers in the music business, a college degree with a broad arts and sciences background and a focus on music (or at least course work including management, communications, contracts and contract law, journalism, law, business, and music) is definitely helpful for success. Possessing a broad range of knowledge about music and the music industry is very important.

On-the-job training will bring the experience needed to promote you in the field. Agents who make arrangements to represent musicians or singers will get a substantial knowledge of the industry through performing in a musical group or working in a recording studio themselves. This also helps to build another important asset—contacts in the music industry. The more, the better.

Desirable personal qualities include salesmanship; good public relations skills; the ability to evaluate and recognize exceptional talent, provide constructive advice, work well with people, gain clients and find appropriate work for them, negotiate successfully, and work at a fast pace and under great pressure; assertiveness (aggressiveness); strong communications skills; excellent phone presence; patience; and perseverance.

For record producers, the most important ability is skill in choosing records that will appeal to many people. A number one hit song is the greatest goal, of course. Thus, successful record producers must be so familiar and comfortable with sound and songs that they are able to pick songs that will do well on the charts. It is important that they can recognize raw talent that can be cultivated when combined with excellent arranging and high quality recording devices.

Business managers need to be cognizant of investments and money strategies.

## EARNINGS

Personal managers usually receive ten to fifteen percent of an artist's earnings. Often, they also receive percentages of merchandise that is sold. They may earn from about $18,000 to $60,000 per year. Naturally, agents wish their clients to be successful because they usually work on a commission basis and if the clients are popular, they will make more money.

Agents for classical musicians usually receive 20 percent for their work in all fields but opera, which receives only a 10 percent commission. In many states, talent agents are licensed.

Booking agents usually take anywhere from 10 to 20 percent of the amount the act is being paid for that performance. In some cases, they are paid a salary plus a percentage of the figures they add to the agency. Amounts vary considerably. but at the top ends they may earn anywhere from $200,000 to $750,000.

Business managers may make $20,000 to $750,000 or more per year. Earnings may be based upon a percentage of the act's total gross income. The percentage varies from 3 to 10 percent.

## CAREER OUTLOOK

The outlook for personal managers and booking agents is cautious. In most cases, individuals begin by representing local talent and work their way up to representing more well-known performers. Since one agent can handle many clients, this is a competitive profession that cannot accommodate large numbers of new people. The best opportunities exist in New York City, Los Angeles, or Nashville.

## STRATEGY FOR FINDING THE JOBS

To break into the booking agent business, work to book the groups in your local area. Make sure the groups understand that you will be taking a percentage of their earnings. Then contact all the possible locations in your area where a group might entertain. You won't make much money but you'll begin to gain the experience you need and make some contacts.

You could also work it the other way by contacting establishments looking for entertainers, working out an agreement, and then finding performers to fill the dates. Be sure to write some kind of a contract to protect everyone involved.

If you are looking to land in a major agency, take any job you can find in the agency, no matter how low on the totem pole. Once you are there, ask questions, do a good job, establish yourself, and look for ways to move up!

# PROFESSIONAL ASSOCIATIONS

Though not a bargaining union, there is an association for personal managers called the Conference of Personal Managers that sets standards of conduct for personal managers.

**Professional Arts Management Institute**
110 Riverside Drive, Suite 4E
New York, NY 10024

**American Institute of Certified Public Accountants (AICPA)**
1211 Avenue of the Americas
New York, NY 10036
Business managers who are accountants may belong to this group.

**Association of Theatrical Press Agents and Managers, AFL–CIO (ATPAM)**
165 West 46th Street
New York, NY 10036

**Conference of Personal Managers (National)**
210 East 51st Street
New York, NY 10019

**Institute of Certified Financial Planners (ICFP)**
7600 East Eastman Avenue, Suite 301
Denver, CO 80231

**International Association of Financial Planning (IAFP)**
Two Concourse Parkway, Suite 800
Atlanta, GA 30328

**Music Distributors Association**
38 West 21st Street, 5th Floor
New York, NY 10010

**National Association of Accountants (NAA)**
10 Paragon Drive
Montvale, NJ 07645

**National Society of Public Accountants (NSPA)**
1010 North Fairfax Street
Alexandria, VA 22314

**Recording Industry Association of America**
1020 19th Street, NW
Washington, DC 20036

---

### MEET BRIAN J. SWANSON

With a BS in Sociology, one in Business Management and another in Industrial Relations from Mankato State University to his credit, Brian J. Swanson acts as president, agent, and accountant of Hello! Booking of Minneapolis, Minnesota.

Previously he worked for several years in retail records; then at Capitol Records; BMG Record Distribution; Glam Slam Nightclub in Minneapolis; and Proton Productions (a booking agency) of Minneapolis.

"I went into the music business fresh out of college in 1986 and started as an agent in 1992," Brian says. "I love the field and enjoy the fact that it also offers me creative input. I am happy that I do not have to wear a suit and I am able to keep in touch with my first passion, music.

"Ninety percent of my day is spent on the phone with artists, record companies, or club buyers. The phone rings about 60 times a day and it is seldom a relaxed environment. There is lots of pressure to perform, which is one of the driving forces behind the success of the company. It is seldom dangerous, unless you count high blood pressure and poor eating habits!

"I like the freedom to work with whomever I choose, provided they are interested in working with me. The hours are terrible! I work about 70-plus hours a week plus the time spent at shows and travel. The plus side is that I have become a big fish in a small Minneapolis pond. The downside is the stress and that I am unsure if I want to try to swim in the big pool. I could get eaten in a day.

"Advising anyone who wants to do this kind of work to *work hard* is the understatement of the year," says Brian. "I would advise that you make sure you have a support network financially just in case

continued

continued

things don't work out. Don't try to do more than one job at a time. In other words, be an agent, or a manager, or a record company, or publicist, or a band member. Don't try to do a couple of things because it probably won't work. You'll end up spreading yourself way too thin and nothing will work for you. One thing is for sure—you must always keep hustling.

"Though I sometimes feel that my career can be a living hell, I absolutely love what I do."

## MEET WAYNE KELLER

Wayne Keller attended Michigan State University in East Lansing, Michigan, majoring in Police Administration and minoring in communications. He now works as an artist's representative in Nashville, Tennessee.

"There is really no training ground or formal education for this profession," says Wayne. "You must first learn the business from its performing standpoint, then from the producer's or club owner's angle. I personally grew up in my father's nightclub in Milwaukee, learned the entertainer's standpoint by "hanging around" with numerous talented performers and by utilizing normal small business practices. My work history prior to becoming an agent was as an office manager for the Pinkerton Detective Agency.

"The most important qualifications for a new agent would be honesty, availability, and the ability to tolerate and nurture the egos of the talented. I was fortunate enough to have learned this by the time I became an agent in 1961 at the age of twenty-nine. I did not, however, have the experience that was almost a prerequisite for becoming an agent, that of having been an entertainer myself. My experience was only from having been an observer of the wonderful world of show business. In fact, to my knowledge, I am the only agent who was not a former entertainer. My former wife was a performer and was definitely a help in handling the helm of the business (as far as staying in touch with the changing sentiments of the various acts and club owners was concerned).

"The profession is really like no other. You go out evenings to watch various people perform and endeavor to have a discussion with them. A few days, weeks, or months later, they write you (submitting photos)

continued

continued

and advise you of their availability on a certain date. You then contact a producer or club owner and inform them of the availability and attributes of the entertainer. (One thing is for sure—there is never anything negative about a performer you are selling.) A contract for that one engagement is then prepared and you go on to the next booking. Once you are established and have instilled confidence in your honesty in both entertainers and clients, the business becomes somewhat routine. You are the catalyst between the acts and their appearances. The atmosphere in the business is always very relaxed and you reach a point where you are paid more for what you know than for the number of hours you work.

"If you're lucky enough to become nationally known and respected, the business almost amounts to making a few telephone calls and instructing your secretary to make up the contracts while you concentrate on obtaining more publicity for your performers.

"The upsides of the business are numerous if you have the ability to do the job. You are constantly dealing with interesting, talented people and behind the scenes of a fascinating field. Your income is restricted only by your own ability. Your schedule is very adaptable and you need only work the hours you choose.

"The downsides include producers and club owners who are not honest with you and do not pay you the agreed-upon fees. And, to some extent, the aforementioned inflated egos of the performers. I must say in defense of these performer egos, however, that they are a necessity. If one is to get up before hundreds of people show after show, night after night, you have to believe in yourself; if your agent chooses to call that an inflated ego, it's his or her problem! For years, I represented two of the greatest nightclub-style performers in the business, comedian–musician Frankie Capri and comedian–singer Nelson Sardelli. Their egos were part of their charm—and they were as good as they believed themselves to be.

"If someone was interested in becoming an agent, he or she should first acquire a working knowledge of show business and 1) be honest, and 2) always be available to your people. You must realize that you are responsible for the livelihood of these entertainers and you must take care of them as your own.

"I was attracted to the business by a love of entertainment, a kind of fascination for the performers, and an awareness of income possibilities that superseded a career as a private detective. Also, in working for yourself you are totally in control of your own destiny in the business world. For me, this translated into thirty wonderful years in this career."

## MEET BILL HIBBLER

Bill Hibbler is owner of Texas Funk Syndicate, an artist management company in Houston, Texas. He attended Houston Community College, in Houston, Texas.

"I've spent twenty-two years in the trenches," says Bill. "I've dealt with vintage guitars, run sound, handled security, been a backline technician, road manager, stage manager, tour coordinator, disc jockey, program director, and album project coordinator. I have also published music industry directories and conducted seminars and managed artists.

"I was always a big fan of music," Bill explains. "As a child, I was always the one who brought the music along. A good friend of mine kept dragging me into music stores to show me the guitar he dreamed of buying. I ended up buying a bass myself but I was never very good at it and gave up after a while. One night after attending a concert, I spotted the salesman who sold me my bass trying to haul about half a dozen guitar cases into the arena for the headliner's guitar player to check out. My friend and I quickly volunteered to help him carry the guitars in and he got us each a stage pass. Once backstage, I was totally fascinated with the whole scene, meeting the bands and watching this small army of technicians and local stagehands break down the gear.

"After that, I was hooked. I spent my afternoons at the venues in the hope that I could help with the instruments or anything else. I freely offered to deliver whatever supplies the crew might need from the music store. Though I didn't make much money, I did get a couple of backstage passes to the shows and would get to meet some of my favorite bands. It wasn't easy at first. I'd have a hard time getting past security and into the arenas, but eventually I developed relationships with the local concert promoters who realized that I was providing a service that was useful to everyone involved. Also, by this time, most of the guitar technicians that were on the road had either met me when they'd been to Houston or had heard of me through the grapevine. I used to make sure to bring a few T-shirts and stickers along (advertising my company), and the stickers would usually find their way onto the bands' flight cases. Word started to get around.

"From the beginning, I knew I wanted to be a road manager. After graduating from high school, I went to college but decided to leave to enter the music business. During the next few years, I ran sound for local bands, booked for a small club, managed a stereo store, and worked at Houston's Agora Ballroom doing security and stage work. In 1982, I got my first break and was hired to be a backline technician for Humble Pie. After a few months, there was a change in management and I became the road manager.

continued

continued

"It was an unusual position to be in at the time. In those days, there were no schools that offered courses in artist or tour management careers and it was difficult to access working tour managers. I'd been in contact with these professionals for years at shows but only briefly, as they were usually very busy. I think the best way to learn this career is to find a mentor and learn what the job is really all about. However, I found myself in the job before finding that mentor. Luckily, I had pretty good instincts, which is important for anyone working on a road crew.

"I spent three great years with Humble Pie before the band broke up. A big mistake I'd made during those years was not developing a better network so that I could find more work. Usually someone in my position would be working for a band with a big management company, booking agent, or record label that would send them out with their other bands or refer them. With Humble Pie, we didn't have that type of management and the band wasn't signed. Our booking agent specialized in southern rock bands like the Allman Brothers, Charlie Daniels Band, and ARS and they kept the same individuals, usually relatives or friends from the early years, without hiring a new crew every time they went out (like a large number of European bands did). I couldn't find a tour manager position so, for several years, I worked as a club disc jockey in Atlanta and later Houston.

"During that time, I met Glenn Hughes when he was about to go out on tour with Black Sabbath. We became friends and he offered me a job as his assistant on the tour. However, Sabbath's management wanted to use someone else at that time. I finally went to work for Glenn in January of 1995 as the project coordinator for his album *Feel.* About six months later, Glenn and his Japanese record label asked me to take over as his manager. I now manage Glenn along with two local bands and am in discussions right now with another established artist.

"My job can be like a roller coaster ride at times. I have to wear a lot of different hats as a manager and some days things are a lot more hectic than others. The time leading up to and during a tour is probably the busiest.

"My work schedule varies tremendously but is always centered around the telephone, fax machine, and e-mail. Glenn's primary markets right now are Europe and Japan so, due to the time difference, I often find myself on the phone as early as five or six A.M. During a tour, I might finish up at nine or ten P.M. by dealing with our tour manager after the show. But there are often gaps in the day where I can get away for a couple of hours if there are no emergencies to deal with.

continued

continued

"Things are a lot more laid back when I direct my attention to studio recording. My initial job is to put a budget together for the album. I'll cut deals with the producer, engineer, and studios for recording, mixing, and mastering; purchase or hire any tape and equipment we'll need; and arrange scheduling, etc. In addition to making arrangements for any supplemental musicians or special guests, I'll take care of arranging photo sessions and meetings with the graphic designer to plan the artwork for both the CD and the marketing materials. (Our label lets us handle a lot of this. Other labels play a much larger role in selecting marketing materials.) During the sessions, I'll be in charge of paying all the bills and tracking expenses. As we get closer to completion, I'll be working with the label to determine promotional plans, schedules, and everything else.

"As to the downsides, I usually enjoy the challenges that arise in the United States, but I find dealing with a European tour to be pretty stressful. It's a lot easier to solve a problem like finding a piece of equipment or a replacement vehicle if the band is here in America where you have easy access to directory assistance and everyone speaks the same language. Even something as simple as finding superglue late at night in Europe is nearly impossible (unlike America where there's a 24-hour convenience store on every corner). In addition to all the usual circumstances, you've got to deal with multiple currencies, which makes for budgeting challenges and bookkeeping problems. There are increased costs of doing business in Europe, obviously phone calls are more expensive, and an overnight envelope costs four times as much to ship. Generally everything from hotels to equipment is costlier and you have to pay value–added taxes as high as 25 percent.

"On the local scene, I've seen so many musicians who will sit and complain about the city they live in, or cut down a rival band that got signed, but never take the necessary steps to make it happen for themselves. At a higher level, there are the people who can't be bothered to show up on time, do interviews, etc., and they step on a lot of people's toes. They forget the old adage about being nice to people on your way up because those same people are going to be there on your way back down. Musicians like that can really be a drain on a manager.

"As far as the upsides/downsides from a more business standpoint, it's not that hard to become a manager. These days, for a few thousand dollars you can put together an office that rivals a big corporation—a computer, modem, printer, telephone with a couple of phone lines and you're in business. Computers really level the playing field because you

continued

continued

can handle your bookkeeping, graphic design, faxing, voice mail, trip planning, mailing lists, contact management, and marketing with one machine. With the Internet and online services you can develop a great network, do research, and market your music without ever leaving your apartment.

"One of the big downsides is that being a manager can become a full-time job long before it pays full-time money. Assuming a typical management commission is 15 percent, your artist has to be grossing $80,000 a year before you can earn $1,000 a month. So at the beginning, it helps to have a day job where you have the ability to make and receive phone calls at work that are band-related.

"For those who might be interested in pursuing this type of work, I would first of all suggest that you read as much as you can about the business. You must acquire a feel for how recording, publishing, and merchandising deals are put together, how record companies and publishing companies are organized, and how things fit into place. You don't have to know how to operate recording and stage gear but it helps to have a good overview of what does what and how the recording process works. And perhaps most important, you need to learn how to understand all the various contracts you'll encounter.

"There are some excellent schools with music business programs but many of them do nothing more than give you a bit of a foundation to build on, rather than enabling you to go right to work. The real education comes from the internship that you should serve while attending school. (If you decide to pursue the school route, I'd recommend doing so in Los Angeles or New York. In those cities you'll have a lot more access to the people who make things happen in the music business than if you choose to take a class back home.) Your school can help you with this and/or you can check online services, music industry forums, and magazines like *LA Music Connection,* which has an intern classified section. Many of these internships require you to be in a school program since you'll probably be working for free and the school internship is the only way a company can get around not paying you minimum wage. That's OK at this point because you'll be gaining valuable experience. I like the idea of interning in a smaller company because in a major record label office, you may be stuck doing phone surveys or in the mail room and never get to really see how things are done.

"Whatever way you choose to get a start on your education, you should treat the music business as a science. Forget about the fantasy of having your band discovered by some A&R guy who fishes your tape out of a pile of demos or who accidentally stumbles into

continued

continued

your show. Set goals, develop a plan for yourself and for your artist, and then take action.

"Besides getting an education, you want to begin developing contacts. It's never too early to start. Keep them in a software program like ACT or Lotus Organizer or in a day planner book. Organize your list of contacts into A, B, and C contacts and prioritize them according to their power and position. Make A the highest level. Call your C-level contacts once every two to three weeks, your B contacts every four to six weeks, and your A contacts once every two to three months and try to find ways to help them while you're trying to help yourself. Learn to be persistent and don't let the word "No" affect you personally. "No" today could mean "Yes" tomorrow. Keep working on and following your game plan, making adjustments as needed. If you make a mistake, try to learn from it—and then move on.

"These days, once you've learned the business, it is entirely possible to find success no matter where you live. Get the right band with the right songs and do what's necessary to release your own CD. Before you release it, follow a preplanned promotional plan and stick to it until you've made a strong impact in your home town. Once your act has reached that level, choose nearby cities or college towns and apply the same plan of action until you accomplish similar results and then continue to expand city by city. Before long, you'll have a nice little region where you're getting airplay at some levels, selling copies of your CD in every city, and are drawing nice crowds to all your shows. Continue to expand in this fashion and the major labels will find you.

"I love to travel, and this business gives me the opportunity to do lots of that, although you often don't get a lot of free time to explore the cities you visit. Still, it's a great adventure. Working in the music business allows me to work at home without facing the boredom of a nine-to-five type job. As a manager, I get to be a part of the big picture and work in a variety of roles. I have friends in the corporate world who are tied to a small section of a huge company. Their role doesn't allow them to see what their contribution is and their work is often duplicated by three or four other people. The trade-off for this used to be job security, but since this is certainly no longer the case, why not take a risk and do something you love? That's what I did!"

# CHAPTER THIRTEEN

# PATH 4: CREATING MUSIC

*The whole problem can be stated quite simply by asking, "Is there a meaning to music?" My answer to that would be, "Yes." And "Can you state in so many words what the meaning is?" My answer to that would be, "No."*

**Aaron Copland**
***What to Listen for in Music***
**(1939), Chapter 2**

B y the age of four, Austrian Wolfgang Amadeus Mozart was studying violin and making up his own compositions. At six, he was traveling the roads of Europe on tour, performing for well-known contemporary musicians and royalty. At eleven, he composed his first opera. At sixteen, he produced four symphonies that established him as one of the leading composers of all time. All together he wrote forty-one symphonies including the well–known *The Marriage of Figaro* in 1787, *Don Giovanni* in 1787, and *The Magic Flute* in 1791. Hardly a typical composer, Mozart's life was ended all too early in 1791.

Though you may not be in Wolfgang's category, composing music may indeed be something that you have a burning desire to do.

## DEFINITION OF THE CAREER PATH

Since music is an ever present part of our lives, this is a career that will never fade from existence. Every day, new music is created—the result of new word combinations and new melodies. Composers and songwriters will always be a part of our world, etching our culture into history and recording it for all generations to come.

## CAREER CHOICES IN CREATING MUSIC

### Composer

Composers are innovative individuals who write music for both instrumentals and vocals in a variety of forms: popular music, classical music, rhythm and blues tunes, symphonies, ballets, operas, radio or television commercials, theme music, background music, sonatas, Broadway music, jazz, country, and many others.

For instance, composers may be hired to write the music for theatrical musical productions or operas. As is the case with any musical production, composers usually work from a script after conferring with the writers, producers, and directors of the show to gain a better understanding and feeling for what the work is all about.

Songs must always fit in with a play's theme. All of the specifications that must be met make this profession a difficult one, especially since all of the people involved must like what the composer has created. If this is not the case, the composer must begin all over again.

### Songwriter

Songwriters may focus on writing melodies, lyrics, or both. Their songs may be designed to be sung by performers at concerts or on CDs; as part of the music for plays, television, or films; or even as radio or television jingles. Songwriters may operate alone or develop a partnership (collaboration) working with another music professional.

There are two basic approaches to writing music. Most songwriters write at specific times during the day or night, establishing a regular routine just as everyone in any profession does. Some songwriters may wait for inspiration and write when the mood or the spirit moves them to write. But this is a risky approach to this profession, especially if you are interested in making a living at it.

Once songs are written, songwriters must officially copyright them through specific governmental agencies. There is another procedure which involves the songwriter placing a finished piece of music in an envelope which is self-addressed, sending it via certified registered mail and keeping it intact without opening it. Most people in the business feel that copyrighting through official channels is much safer.

Songwriters must not only write songs, they must learn to be effective at marketing them. Nothing is gained if that is not accomplished, because there can be no "hit" songs for songs that never get heard.

In order to get attention for a song, the songwriter will make up demos and send them to people who might be in a position to further the song's potential. Prior to sending these out, it is recommended that a query letter be sent that highlights the features of the song and peaks the reader's interest. If successful, the song may be accepted by a recording group, music publishers, or some other individual associated with the music business who can promote the song in some way.

## Arranger

Arrangers are faced with the task of changing an existing piece of music by placing the melody in a particular order to create new harmonies and alter and improve the rhythms. Arranging may be performed for any musical instrument. Proficient arrangers will rework a song with current trends in mind to try to turn it into a hit. They may work for music services like Muzak, for music publishers, in television, or in the motion picture industry. Sometimes, established musicians move on to become arrangers, often working as freelance professionals.

## POSSIBLE JOB TITLES

| | | |
|---|---|---|
| Adapter | Lyricist | Transcripter |
| Arranger | Songwriter | Writer |
| Composer | Transcriber | |

## POSSIBLE EMPLOYERS

Geographically, it is possible to write songs in any area of the country, actually any area of the world. However, staff positions through producers, recording groups, or recording companies are more easily secured in cities like Los Angeles, New York, or Nashville.

For talented composers who are looking to begin a career writing for musical productions, prospects exist in smaller theaters and production companies. Otherwise, you must look to team up with someone who will be willing to finance the project.

Once composers have established a reputation, they may be approached by producers to write the music for projects. Composers who have achieved good reviews will be offered additional projects.

## RELATED OCCUPATIONS

| | |
|---|---|
| Communications expert | Music editor |
| Conductor | Music librarian |
| Copyist | Music teacher |
| Creative writer for advertising or marketing | Music writer |
| | Orchestrator |
| Fiction writer | Performer |
| Grant writer | Recording industry employee |
| Music critic | Retail music salesperson |

## WORKING CONDITIONS

Composers and arrangers often do much of their work as solitary endeavors. Usually the workplace is one's home or studio.

Since those who engage in this kind of work must often juggle a number of projects all at one time, they may be required to work days, evenings, weekends, and even holidays if deadlines must be met. In order to accomplish this, a great deal of discipline and planning are required and stress must be overcome.

Composers and songwriters may put in a large number of hours without any guarantee of monetary or personal reward.

This kind of work can be done on a full-time or part-time basis.

## TRAINING AND QUALIFICATIONS

Though no formal education may be required to become a songwriter, composer, or arranger, a great deal of knowledge, expertise, and musical ability are required to be successful in these careers. Often, those interested in doing this kind of work attend colleges, universities, conservatories, and major in music and/or theater arts. Studying music theory, orchestration, and harmony are valuable. Often, musical training has begun at an early age and proficiency on at least one instrument has been accomplished.

To build towards a career as a composer, experts advise that you become familiar with all kinds of productions involving music, listen to a variety of Broadway musicals and operas, write for school and/or local productions, find a related internship (also check with local production companies to see if they provide any kind of workshops or other training vehicles), and work in summer stock or regional theater productions. Experience in writing poetry may also come in handy.

Music conferences, workshops, and the like will also increase an individual's expertise in composing and arranging. Both experience and contacts are gained when arranging music for others or through working as a copyist (one who does transcribing). Other possibilities include playing an instrument in a professional arena such as in a band or symphony or applying for a grant from the National Endowment of the Arts (NEA).

On a personal level, composers need to be creative, disciplined, musically talented, persistent, and patient. Also required is sufficient business acumen, worthwhile music contacts, knowledge of instruments, and adaptability. Good timing and a measure of good luck are also pluses.

## EARNINGS

Since most composers and arrangers are self-employed, it is important to factor in the reality that they must provide their own benefits, including health insurance, vacation time, and pension. They must also absorb expenses such as copying fees, traveling costs, mailings, and organizational dues that can amount to several thousand dollars per year.

For established composers, payments or royalties are often earned every time their work is performed or published. Composers share with producers who receive half of performance royalties.

Though earnings will vary, the following list provides a range of figures:

Film score: Up to $30,000
Half-hour television show: Up to $2,500
Television movie: $12,000 to $15,000
Television four-hour miniseries: Up to $30,000
Lyricist, per song: Up to $8,000

Yearly salaries will depend on a number of factors—how many songs are published or sold, how popular the song is, how many times it is being played, and the agreement reached for each tune. As is the case with books, songs may be sold for one flat fee or be subject to royalties to the publisher and/or writer. If songs are the result of collaborations, the total earnings will be split evenly between the two parties involved. Very successful songwriters may be in the $500,000 to a million dollars per year category. However, it is also quite conceivable to earn $1,000 to $8,000.

## CAREER OUTLOOK

Competition is so keen that the outlook for those interested in this career is not very promising. However, with talent, patience, and perseverance, one can succeed.

## STRATEGY FOR FINDING THE JOBS

Start writing songs, if you haven't already—no matter how old you are. Find others who enjoy your work. Join musical, youth, school, local community groups, and professional associations. Make as many contacts as you can. Volunteer to write something for free—perhaps a local school's fight song or a seasonal tune for your community.

## PROFESSIONAL ASSOCIATIONS

**Academy of Country Music (ACM)**
P.O. Box 508
Hollywood, CA 90078

**American Composers Alliance**
170 West 74th Street
New York, NY 10023

**American Society of Composers and Publishers (ASCAP)**
1 Lincoln Plaza
New York, NY 10023

**American Society of Music Copyists (ASMC)**
Box 2557
Times Square Station
New York, NY 10108

**Composers Recording, Inc.**
170 West 74th Street
New York, NY 10023

**Meet the Composer, Inc.**
2112 Broadway, Suite 505
New York, NY 10023

**Nashville Songwriters Association International (NSAI)**
803 Eighteenth Street South
Nashville, TN 37203

**National Association of Composers, USA (NACUSA)**
P.O. Box 49652
Barrington Station
Los Angeles, CA 90049

**The Songwriters Guild**
276 Fifth Avenue
New York, NY 10001

## MEET McNEIL JOHNSTON

McNeil Johnston grew up in Honolulu, Hawaii, and then attended Mannes College of Music in New York, majoring in Music Theory and Music Composition. Today he serves as a partner and the musical director of Outland Productions.

"I've been a musician all my life," says McNeil, "Piano since age four, violin since age ten, composing for orchestra by the sixth grade. There was never any question in my heart as to my overall career choice. I decided in college that composition suited me best—aspiring to an instrumental performance career was too much pressure, too much work (and practice!) and a bit too limiting creatively.

"My job is one of constant variety. Any given moment may find me orchestrating another composer's work, recording a jingle or two, writing my own music, or scoring a video. Typically, I'm up at 6:30 A.M. I act as both Mr. Mom and Mr. Music as I try to work in my basement studio while seeing to my two daughters' needs and whims. Late at night (between 10:00 P.M. and 2:00 A.M.), I put in many additional hours while the family is asleep.

"I write a lot of commercially oriented music using MIDI technology because I've found that it's a very efficient and speedy way to 'write.'

continued

continued

I play parts into the sequencer, edit in the computer, and voila—music! Busy? Relaxed? Both!

"I love the fact that I get work in spurts—feast or famine. I thrive on tight deadlines and doing the 'impossible.' I enjoy working at home using my own equipment for the most part, though I am occasionally found in larger recording studios. I work as much as is necessary, so the amount of hours per week varies between zero and 100!

"What I love about my work is that it's my work! As a composer/ orchestrator, I put my stamp on everything I do. It's about as close to pure creativity as you can get and still get paid for doing it! What I don't like is that I'm occasionally wide open to criticism by the musically challenged. I've had a couple of what I call come-backers: orchestrations or compositions that were rejected for silly reasons that have very little to do with music.

"I'd advise other aspiring composers and songwriters to keep plugging, praying, preparing, practicing, and perspiring. Also, never never never even pretend you think you might know everything there is to know about what you do. Remember, there's a word for the moment we stop learning...DEATH!"

## MEET JEFFREY WINSTON MIKULSKI

Jeffrey Winston Mikulski is a composer, sound designer, and owner of Climbing Ivy Media.

"I started playing guitar in high school and went on to play in clubs," says Jeffrey. "I have muscular dystrophy, so running around town was becoming increasingly more difficult. After receiving my BA in Communications from State University College at Buffalo, I decided I wanted a music degree, so I went on and earned a two-year music degree from a private college and am now in the slow progress of getting a BFA.

"Somewhere along the line I became interested in composition and started building a project studio. That led me to scoring and sound design plays and later other forms. I became more interested in this kind of work and so have placed my focus there.

"I wrote my first theater score in 1991 and established my company on December 4, 1995. I had been writing electronic compositions for a year or so, and my most common reaction was 'that sounds like something from a movie.' As I began to pay more attention to film scores, I

continued

continued

was intrigued by the range of the music and how it was used to convey different emotions. It was a kind of 'world building.' It w ent beyond the stylistic limits of any one genre of music and sometimes, music altogether. I've been asked to create the sound of things and places that don't exist outside of the audience's imagination. It can be very creative.

"A typical day breaks down into two categories—working or looking for work. When you are hired, it's usually very hectic. Audio tends to be the last thing added, so lead times are very short. Actually, I've experienced twenty-four-hour working days and eighty-hour weeks fairly often. I actually have a lot of control over my time, especially within a given day. However, when there's a deadline, it's got to be done by that date and that's that.

"When not actively engaged in a particular project, my time is spent either making calls trying to find the next project or maintaining and updating my studio. You can't be too experimental with your method with a week to work, so you do it in between gigs. I create sounds or SFXs and learn new software, always looking for ways to speed up the process. Also, I have to maintain basic music skills, too, so I practice instruments and study theory. I have to be able to create music that sounds like any and all styles from all over the world. To do that, I have to first learn what they are. These days are much more relaxed, basic eight-hour types, nice but I really enjoy the push, too.

"To start a project I usually talk with the director or whoever is creatively in charge to get an idea of the mood or feel of the project. Then I go back to my studio and gather my resources. I produce some basic pieces, sample sounds, or create rough designs. At the level I'm at now, I do everything—score, orchestrate, record, engineer, plus all the basic business and administrative tasks.

"Hopefully by this point, I get a cue sheet listing the SFX and music cues and their approximate times. If I can, I attend rehearsals and try to get a vision of the piece. The director and I meet again to hear the things I've planned and I listen to their feedback. From then on, it's a matter of refining and meeting the changes they find during rehearsals. When all is set, I go back to my studio and write and record the final pieces. Unfortunately, this must often happen in a matter of days. There isn't much time to come up with new ideas so you have to learn to be good—fast.

"I love the fact that I do project work; everything is different from the last thing you did. I get to be around bright, creative people who have a lot of passion for what they do. The work is quite difficult, so if y ou ae doing it, it's because this is where you want to be.

continued

continued

"The down side? Pay is not always great and the dry spells can be a little scary. Some jobs are less than inspiring but they keep up cash flow. I deal with a lot of technology that occasionally does not behave. Having a piece of gear go down in the middle of a project can be a real nightmare, and one you can't get away from because the work has to get done, period.

"Probably the worst thing, though, is the feeling that I could have done something a little better if I had more time. Everything that goes out seems unfinished. I guess that will never change.

"As far as recommendations go, I would say that obviously you need a well-thought-out career path with a good education. Sound design is becoming part of the curriculum in some colleges. I would also advise that you try to get to where things are happening—New York and Los Angeles are two of those places. And make sure that this is what you want. If it is, then go for it. Learn everything you can. Find people who are in the business and ask questions. I've found that most people are very approachable. Decide what your specialty will be and develop that. There are a lot of people doing this and you have to have something unique to your work. Study everything, especially other art forms. My fiancée is a fine artist. Learning how a painter thinks and applying that metaphor taught me how to compose. Study people and life. Everything you experience comes out in your creative work.

"I am grateful to be part of a process that creates something out of nothing. Though it can be nerve wracking, the feeling of accomplishment is great. To those who wish to join me in this noble profession, I say *Good Luck!*"

# CHAPTER FOURTEEN

# PATH 5:
# TEACHING MUSIC

*A teacher affects eternity; no one can tell where his influence stops.*

## Henry Adams

The ancient philosophers Plato and Aristotle endorsed music as an important aspect of a good citizen's life. In many ancient civilizations, music was considered a vital social activity. In Greece, for example, children were taught to sing, play lyres, flutes, and harps at an early age. Today's music educators follow in this path.

## DEFINITION OF THE CAREER PATH

Did you have a teacher who inspired you to seek a path as a music educator? Often, people attribute their career goals, at least in part, to teachers who served as role models. Perhaps you can serve in this capacity for others who will become your students.

In the field of music, teaching is a career that allows individuals who are very knowledgeable about a particular instrument (including the voice) to share their appreciation and expertise with others.

## CAREER CHOICES IN TEACHING MUSIC

### School Music Teacher

The ultimate goal for all music educators is to provide the children with a love for and an interest in music. To this end, they plan musical programs, encourage the children to participate, coordinate musical activities with other school functions or perhaps activities in the community at large.

Music teachers in both public and private schools may be responsible for teaching music appreciation, history, literature, and theory to students at any level—kindergarten through high school. In addition, educators may organize and direct school orchestras, choral groups, and other school-related music activities.

In elementary schools, music teachers may be responsible for teaching music in one school or several schools in the district, meeting once or several times a week. In the early grades, teachers are expected to focus on rhythm. Often they use marching and clapping to establish interest in this area. At this level, simple instruments such as recorders and rhythm instruments are used. The teacher may bring in a guitar to share music and songs with the children.

Administrative duties may include purchasing musical instruments, equipment, music books, and sheet music. Additional responsibilities include keeping the musical equipment in shape, preparing budgets for musical programs, writing lesson plans and objectives, and evaluating the music programs and the progress of the students. Teachers are always called upon to attend meetings, serve on committees, meet with parents, work with students who have individual needs, supervise extracurricular projects, and meet other obligations dictated by the principal or the school board.

Some music teachers may entertain at functions and write their own songs and try to market them.

## Independent Music Teacher/Private Instrument or Voice Teacher

---

**HELP WANTED**

**Piano Teachers.** Suburbs and south side of city only. Must work well with students and adults at all ages and all levels. Please call: (964) 555-2211.

---

Teachers who give private lessons and who are self-employed have more freedom to set up their teaching programs as they wish. They may prefer to work with one student or several at a time. Some individuals find a site from which to teach or offer these services through their homes. In other cases, the teachers travel to pupils' homes.

Successful private teachers must be able to make the experience enjoyable and informative for the students, allowing them to build their skills and love for music in the process.

Teachers often schedule recitals for family and friends. This provides an opportunity for the students to work towards a goal, display their musical talents and effort, and raise their self-esteem for a job well done.

Teaching may be done on a full-time basis or in conjunction with a full- or part-time music position (or other occupation). Those who decide to do this kind of work need to build a clientele to make it worthwhile. Teachers charge anywhere from $15 per lesson on up.

## College, University or Conservatory Music Educator

Assistant professors, associate professors, and professors serve as music educators in colleges, universities, or conservatories. They may be responsible for teaching general music, music theory, music history, or instrumental and/or vocal performance. Other possibilities include conducting choruses or orchestras and publishing articles relating to the field.

Educators employed by community colleges usually teach approximately eighteen hours per week while those at four-year colleges or universities usually teach approximately nine to twelve hours per week. Add to that the typical responsibilities of all teachers—preparation time, meetings, school events, availability to students, serving on committees, grading papers and exams, and evaluating students' progress in general. Total working hours probably number in excess of forty-five hours per week.

## POSSIBLE JOB TITLES

| | |
|---|---|
| College music teacher | Private music teacher |
| Educator | Private school music teacher |
| Independent music teacher | Public school music teacher |
| Instructor | School music teacher |
| Music coach | Secondary music teacher |
| Private instrument or | Studio teacher |
| voice teacher | Substitute teacher |

## POSSIBLE EMPLOYERS

Since both public and private schools employ music teachers, the possibility of employment exists at all schools at all levels—elementary, secondary, and college level as well as at music conservatories. Added to this are adult education programs and the possibility of teaching private lessons.

# RELATED OCCUPATIONS

Some of the same skills used by teachers are used by individuals in the following occupations:

| | |
|---|---|
| Author | Guidance counselor |
| Coach | Librarian |
| Composer | Museum curator |
| Consultant | Researcher |
| Counselor | Sales representative |
| Editor | Social worker |

# WORKING CONDITIONS

Music educators work in a school setting where they may be assigned to an ordinary classroom or a music room that has been equipped with specially designed acoustics that help the music teacher define and enrich the sound of the children's voices. The specially designed room may have semicircular risers or platforms. Rehearsals for chorus, orchestra, or band ensembles will be held here and led by the music teacher also.

Substantial time may be spent in other places, such as an assembly hall when special musical productions are offered or out-of-doors if the teacher's specific responsibilities call for this.

While those teaching in public or private schools may maintain a fairly normal schedule, those who give private lessons may have more irregular hours because of the necessity of working within the schedules of busy students and adults.

# TRAINING AND QUALIFICATIONS

All public school music teachers must achieve state certification, which can be met through a bachelor's degree in music education at an accredited college or university. It is possible to teach at some private schools without certification although this is becoming more and more rare.

Typical courses at the undergraduate level would include:

Background for Teaching Music in Elementary School

Background for Teaching Music in High School

Child Development

Conducting

Chorus

Educational Psychology

Group Voice

Form and Analysis

Orchestration

Piano Musicianship

Public Performance

Student Teaching

Some states may require a master's degree, even at the elementary or secondary level. Teaching at a college or conservatory always requires at least a master's degree. Many demand a doctoral degree. In addition, most positions require previous teaching experience.

On a personal level, it is important for teachers at all levels to be capable of working well with people, to have an aptitude for conveying an enthusiasm about music to others, and to have the ability to teach others what you already know. You will need to be skilled in playing at least one instrument (preferably more), have good communication skills, be independent, have initiative, a good sense of humor, intellectual skills, patience, and flexibility.

For teachers giving private music lessons, it is necessary to have extensive training or study on a particular instrument or instruments—usually piano plus another instrument. In addition, they must possess the skills necessary to teach someone else how to play an instrument or sing with greater proficiency. Personal qualities include patience, good communications skills, and a true love of music.

## $E$ARNINGS

Typical earnings for educators are listed below:

Public school: $18,000 to $50,000
Private school: $16,000 to $35,000
Individual lessons: $10 to $30 per hour ($12,000 to $30,000 plus
    per year)

continued

continued

Conservatory: $25,000 to $70,000

College/University

Instructor: $25,000 to $37,000 (nine to twelve teaching hours)

Assistant Professor: $35,000 to $50,000 (Ph.D. level) (nine to twelve teaching hours)

Associate Professor: $50,000 to $60,000 (Ph.D. level) (six to nine teaching hours plus supervision of doctoral students)

Full Professor: $60,000 to $80,000 (Ph.D. level) (three to six teaching hours plus supervision of doctoral students and publication required)

Usually benefits for teachers are good and job security (after establishing tenure) is assured. Typical benefits include:

❑ Hospitalization and other medical coverage

❑ Dental coverage

❑ Paid vacations

❑ Paid holidays

❑ Bonuses

❑ Life insurance

❑ Disability insurance

❑ 401K or other financial vehicle

❑ Tuition reimbursement

## CAREER OUTLOOK

Opportunities for music educators continue to increase as the popularity of music is spurred by new media techniques. On the other hand, when there are educational cutbacks, the music departments may be among the first to be hit. Positions at the college, university, and conservatory level are not easy to come by and competition for available positions is very stiff.

Prospects are always good for talented teachers who wish to give private, semiprivate, or group lessons. Word of mouth travels fast once someone is happy with their instructor or their child's instructor. When just starting out, you could contact music and instrument shops in your area and elucidate your credentials. Ask if they would be willing to recommend you to individuals seeking lessons. Have business cards made up that can be passed out at the retail establishments. Also contact public and private schools and religious organizations in your neighborhood to establish your credentials with them. Best targets for jobs would be large cities and metropolitan areas with enough people to warrant several private teachers.

## Strategy for Finding the Jobs

### Be Aware of Teacher Certification Requirements

Make sure you are aware of all teacher certification requirements so there are no unpleasant "surprises." Attend a school that will give you the credentials you need for state certification. Some positions will require that you get a master's degree and/or take a proficiency exam.

### Take Advantage of School Placement Services and Approach School Systems Directly

Work through your school's placement service and also approach school systems directly. Have your resume and cover letter ready. (Include your philosophy of music education. Why is it important?) If they have no openings now, ask them to keep your credentials on file in case an opening occurs. Summer sessions may provide a good opportunity for you to get your foot in the door.

### Check Newspapers, Employment Agencies, and the Internet

Other avenues for finding jobs include reading the weekly want ads (they are available at most libraries), investigating employment agencies (some specialize in working with teachers), and surfing the Internet. The World Wide Web (WWW) has a vast number of areas that offer career advice and provide information about job openings and further contacts.

### Job Fairs

Job fairs that focus on educational possibilities may provide you with knowledge of openings or contacts for future positions.

### Special Contacts for Positions at Higher Levels of Education

Those who seek positions at institutions of higher learning (and who have earned a Ph.D.) will probably need to prepare a curriculum vitae (C.V.) instead of or in addition to a resume. This vehicle stresses your interests, experience, publications, and achievements in research. A good resource to help you prepare this is VGM Career Horizons *How to Prepare Your Curriculum Vitae.*

For positions at the college, university, or conservatory level, you may obtain a list of openings called the *Music Faculty List* provided by the College Music Society (CMS) and the American Musicological Society (AMS). The list is available to members. The *Chronicle of Higher Education* also publishes a weekly newspaper that features a list of faculty positions available in colleges and universities. In addition, you should approach institutions of higher learning directly.

## Special Resources

*Peterson's Guide to Independent Secondary Schools* and the *Handbook of Private Schools* are two excellent resources to avail yourself of. They are published by Porter Sargent Publishers of Boston. Another helpful resource is *Independent School,* a publication of the *Journal of the National Association of Independent Schools,* which is published three times yearly. Other resources include *Current Jobs for Graduates in Education,* the *Job Hunter, Community Jobs, Current Jobs for Graduates,* and *Patterson's American Education* and *Patterson's Elementary Education* published by Educational Directories.

# PROFESSIONAL ASSOCIATIONS

**American Federation of Teachers of the United States and Canada**
1501 Broadway, Suite 600
New York, NY 10036

**American Federation of Teachers (AFT)**
555 New Jersey Avenue, N.W.
Washington, DC 20001

**American Musicological Society (AMS)**
University of Pennsylvania
201 South 34th Street
Philadelphia, PA 19104

**College Band Directors National Association**
University of Texas
Box 8028
Austin, TX 78713

**College Music Society (CMS)**
202 West Spruce
Missoula, MT 59802

**Music Educators National Conference**
1806 Robert Fulton Drive
Reston, VA 22091

**Music Teacher National Association**
617 Vine Street, Suite 505
Cincinnati, OH 45202

**National Association of College Wind and Percussion Instructors (NACWPI)**
Northeast Missouri State University
Division of Fine Arts
Kirksville, MO 63501

**National Association of Schools of Music**
11250 Roger Bacon Drive, Suite 21
Reston, VA 22091

**Society for Music Teacher Education**
1806 Robert Fulton Drive
Reston, VA 22091

---

### MEET CHRIS GOEKE

Chris Goeke is Assistant Professor of Voice at Southeast Missouri State University in Cape Girardeau, Missouri. Her background includes a BA in Music and an MA/DMA in Voice Performance and Pedagogy. Added to that are private coaching with voice teachers and coaches in New York City and classes and workshop performances in New York City.

"Coming from a musical family, I have always been involved with music in some way," says Chris. "I started by playing trumpet in junior high school. In high school, I started performing in summer musicals. This was really important because I then began identifying myself as a performer. During college I worked as a shop assistant in the opera department. When I was working on my master's degree, I was an assistant voice teacher. During and after my formal education, I gained experience in a whole range of performing including a large amount of church and synagogue work (primarily over the weekends), considerable chorus work, also singing small parts and participating in concerts. In 1990, I was an adjunct professor at Grinnell College and a teaching assistant at the University of Iowa.

continued

continued

"For the position I now have, you need a doctorate degree in voice; skills in singing; a voice that people find pleasing; teaching experience; good organizational and planning skills; the ability to communicate effectively one-on-one; good piano skills (preferably at least intermediate); awareness of musical styles such as opera, art songs, and musical theater; and the ability to speak another language along with good language skills in Spanish, Italian, German, and Russian. In addition, you must enjoy researching music, must be sensitive to various personality styles, and understand voice development over the course of four years.

"I usually work from about 8:15 A.M. until about 5:00 P.M., says Chris. "A week's work usually amounts to about 50 hours, with hours devoted in the evenings and at least one day every weekend. Early mornings are generally spent with preparatory work and/or planning. I have one or two hours of classroom instruction along with three hours of individual instruction. Time is also spent in rehearsals for myself or a school activity. And of course no day would be complete without a meeting or two. Evening hours are filled with grading, planning, rehearsals, attending concerts, etc. When it comes time to prepare for a show, I work with the orchestra and theater department and things really get busy!

"I have my own office, which has a piano/desk, nice audio, video, and stereo equipment. This is uncommon and came about because I received a grant for researching how audio/video equipment play a role in voice lessons. The work office is relaxed and congenial for the most part and I am free to do what I feel is needed. I have minimal supervision. However, I am evaluated twice a year by the faculty and at the end of every course by the students.

"I like the freedom involved in this job and the fact that I am working in a field that I enjoy. I like being creative. What I like least are the hours (evenings and weekends) and the unpredictability. You can only get a half semester planned. The pay is okay, but it could be better.

"To others who are considering getting into this field, I would say to make sure that wherever you decide to go to school, you'll be able to communicate and learn from your teacher. You need to have good one-on-one voice training. Your decision as to whom you will train with will affect your musical style and teaching ability in the years to come. I would also stress that I feel that professional experience is really helpful. Don't get all your training in a formal setting. By getting out there you will gain more practical and beneficial experience—the more and varied the experience, the better. This will provide you with a good solid foundation for the future.

continued

continued

"Teaching and performing are very gratifying. Watching your students transform as people and performers over the course of years is also very rewarding. People enter into music careers for different reasons—some for money, experience, or because they truly enjoy it. It's a difficult business to be in unless you really want it. You have to view it as something worth sticking with. And if you want to achieve any measure of success, you'll have to pay your dues, and work your way up the ladder."

# CHAPTER FIFTEEN

# PATH 6: MUSIC RETAILING, WHOLESALING, AND REPAIR

*Music has charms to soothe a
savage breast,
To soften rocks, or bend a
knotted oak.*

William Congreve,
*The Mourning Bride*

## CAREER CHOICES IN MUSIC RETAILING, WHOLESALING, AND REPAIR

**HELP WANTED**

**Record label seeks individuals** for marketing, public relations, sales, and internships. Need reliable, motivated candidates. Advancement and management future. Please call (965) 555-4567.

**Marketing/Sales—Midwest.** Music/sound design company seeking enthusiastic self-starter to handle in-house marketing, client services, and agency sales calls.

continued

**Need organized, flexible person** to handle multiple projects, promptly respond to client requests, and meet deadlines. Salary plus commission and benefits. Please fax resume to (888) 555-0097.

**Can you sell?** Do you know musical instruments/pro-audio gear? Would you like to work in a high energy sales environment with other motivated team-oriented people? Then the Music Center may be the place for you! Immediate openings in sales. Management openings also available. Apply in person at 1233 Worth Street.

**Independent Record Label** seeks motivated individuals to join our team. Knowledge of underground music is necessary as well as strong communication and computer skills. Previous label experience preferred. Current openings in our sales/marketing, order entry/fulfillment, publicity/promotions, and Internet departments. Well-rounded, aggressive, highly motivated, and energetic applicants only. Also looking to fill position at our retail location. Previous music, retail/marketing experience preferred with strong background in all underground genres. Fax resumes to (444) 555-4569.

**Symphony Orchestra.** Our exciting 1997–1998 telephone fundraising campaign has begun. A few positions are still open for enthusiastic and articulate people. Great job—great pay. Part time. Please call (754) 555-9067.

Professionals who serve in the music industry in the areas of music retailing and wholesaling share their knowledge of musical products and the music business in general in an effort to serve people's needs, solve their problems, and help them select the product that is right for them. Those who repair musical instruments and equipment make sure that individuals can continue to use the musical equipment they have become accustomed to—also a very important responsibility.

The category of music retailing and wholesaling is a wide area that encompasses working in music stores, operating as a manufacturer's representative, or serving in any music-related establishment that offers goods or services to the public. Repair is also a large area open to those who have expertise in music and great familiarity with the piano and/or other musical instruments.

## Music Retailing

It is important that all sales professionals know their merchandise and the music business in general, be cognizant of selling techniques, and work well with a variety of people. They must be knowledgeable, patient, organized, detail-minded, and responsible.

For those who are interested in music retail, there are many options. If you prefer a smaller scale enterprise, you may be responsible for dealing with customers, packing and unpacking merchandise at designated intervals, taking inventory, keeping records, writing up sales receipts, handling payment of goods purchased, ordering stock, and restocking shelves. In a larger store, your assignments are apt to be more specific and with fewer responsibilities; for instance, you may be expected to only sell the merchandise and send the customer to a payment window to complete the transaction.

Typical merchandise in a music establishment includes:

band and orchestra instruments

guitars and banjos

pianos and organs

cassette tapes

compact discs (CDs)

stereo sound equipment

electronic instruments

sheet music

music books

videotapes

music videos

computer-generated sound equipment

music accessories

musical equipment

If you desire to work your way up the ladder into a management position, you will be responsible for carrying out the policies of the owner or the corporation. As a manager, typically your duties will include hiring new personnel and training them, supervising all of their activities, preparing the orders for new merchandise, putting together all of the store displays, creating and implementing sales campaigns, placing advertising, and dealing with and settling customer problems satisfactorily.

## Music Wholesaling

Operating on a wholesale level, music or instrument sales representatives approach retail stores and other outlets with the merchandise they have to offer from the specific labels or manufacturers they represent. The merchandise will probably include CDs, tapes, cassettes, and videos. Those who represent instrument companies offer their musical instruments and supplies to shops, schools, and dealerships. Usually they are assigned a particular area or district or even a client base, from which they travel selling their products and/or services. As such, they are usually required to meet specific quotas. Those who are good at this can do very well financially—upwards of $65,000 per year.

Wholesale sales representatives may also be in charge of inventory, setting up in-store displays, keeping client records, and making sure that all of their customers' needs are being met. In addition, they must attend meetings and follow up on all details.

## Music Repair

### Piano Technicians (Piano Tuners and Repairers).
There are about 10,000 professionals who work as instrument and piano repairers/tuners. Included in this group are pipe organ tuners along with those who repair brass, woodwind, percussion, or stringed instruments.

Piano tuners are entrusted with the responsibility of adjusting piano strings to the proper pitch. A standard 88-key piano that has 230 strings can usually be tuned properly in about an hour and a half. This is how it's done: A string's pitch is the frequency at which it vibrates and produces sound when it is struck by one of the piano's wooden hammers. Tuners begin the process by adjusting the pitch of the "A" string by striking the key and comparing the string's pitch with that of the tuning fork. To make the pitch match that of the tuning fork, the tuner uses a tuning hammer (also called a tuning lever or wrench) and turns a steel pin to tighten or loosen the string. Then the pitch of every string is set in relation to the "A" string.

A piano has thousands of wooden, steel, iron, ivory, and felt parts that can be plagued by an assortment of problems. To correct what might be wrong, piano repairers speak with customers to get an idea of what is not functioning properly. Then repairers will begin to dismantle the piano to inspect the parts. Using common hand tools as well as specially designed ones (tools for repining and restringing, for example), repairers will replace old or worn parts, realign moving parts that have shifted, or do whatever is necessary, even completely rebuild the piano. Since there are so many parts, made of so many materials, piano repairers have their work cut out for them.

In addition to repair work, piano repairers may also tune pianos. This requires knowledge of the use of specialized tools, as well as a "good ear."

**Pipe Organ Repairers.**   Pipe organ repairers tune, repair, and install organs that make music by forcing air through flue pipes or reed pipes. The flue pipe sounds when a current of air strikes a metal lip in the side of the pipe. The reed pipe sounds when a current of air vibrates a brass reed inside the pipe.

To tune an organ, repairers first match the pitch of the "A" pipes with that of a tuning fork. The pitch of other pipes is set by comparing it to that of the "A" pipes. To tune a flue pipe, repairers move the metal slide, which increases or decreases the pipe's "speaking length." To tune a reed pipe, the tuner alters the length of the brass reed. Most organs have hundreds of pipes, so often a day or more is needed to completely tune an organ.

Pipe organ repairers locate problems, repair or replace worn parts, and clean pipes. Repairers also assemble organs on-site in churches and auditoriums, following manufacturer's blueprints. They use hand and power tools to install and connect the air chest, blowers, air ducts, pipes, and other components. They may work in teams or be assisted by helpers. Depending on the size of the organ, a job may take several weeks or even months.

**Violin Repairers.**   Violin repairers adjust and repair bowed instruments such as violins, violas, and cellos, using a variety of hand tools. Defects are uncovered by inspecting and playing the instruments. Then, repairers remove cracked or broken sections, repair or replace defective parts. They also sand rough spots, fill in scratches with putty, and apply paint or varnish.

**Guitar Repairers.**   Guitar repairers inspect and play the instrument to determine defects. They replace levels using hand tools, and fit wood or metal parts. They reassemble and string guitars.

**Brass and Woodwind Instrument Repairers.**   Brass and woodwind instrument repairers clean, repair, or adjust all brass and woodwind instruments including trumpets, coronets, French horns, trombones, tubas, clarinets, flutes, saxophones, oboes, and bassoons. They move mechanical parts or play scales to find defects. They may unscrew and remove rod pins, keys, and pistons and remove soldered parts using gas torches. They repair dents in metal instruments using mallets or burnishing tools. They fill cracks in wood instruments by inserting pinning wire and covering them with filler. Repairers also inspect instrument keys and replace worn pads and corks.

Percussion instrument repairers work on drums, cymbals, and xylophones. In order to repair a drum, they remove drum tension rod screws and rods by hand or by using a drum key. They cut new drumheads from animal skin, stretch the skin over rim hoops, and tuck it around and under the hoop using hand-tucking tools. To prevent a crack in a cymbal, gong, or similar instrument from advancing, repairers may operate a drill press or hand power drill to drill holes at the inside edge of the crack. Another technique they may use involves cutting out sections around the cracks using shears or grinding wheels. They also replace the bars and wheels of xylophones.

## POSSIBLE JOB TITLES

| | |
|---|---|
| Brass and woodwind instrument repairer | Organ repairer |
| | Piano repairer |
| Guitar repairer | Piano technician |
| Instrument repairer | Piano tuner |
| Instrument restorer | Pipe organ repairer |
| Instrument sales representative | Regional sales manager |
| Manufacturer's representative | Sales manager |
| Music sales clerk | Salesperson |
| Music shop manager | Violin repairer |

## POSSIBLE EMPLOYERS

Those interested in music sales at the wholesale or retail level may contact local music stores or other music enterprises, music factories, company headquarters, or dealers.

Major and independent music companies employ large numbers of salespeople in all music markets—the largest are located in Detroit, Atlanta, Chicago, Los Angeles, Nashville, New York City, Memphis, Philadelphia, Jacksonville, Baltimore, and Miami among others.

Eight out of ten music repairers and tuners work in music stores, and most of the rest work in repair shops, for musical instrument manufacturers, or are self-employed. Other possibilities include music schools, conservatories, colleges and universities, music shops, or music groups. Large cities offer the greatest opportunities. Those who are self-employed may gain additional clients through advertising, word of mouth, or through contracts or other arrangements worked out between them and schools or associations.

## RELATED OCCUPATIONS

The skills involved in retailing instruments and other musical supplies are the same used to sell any type of product or service. This would include the following careers:

Advertising account executive      Insurance agent
Appliance sales      Real estate agent
Computer salesperson      Telemarketing
Furniture salesperson      Travel agent

Additional possible related occupations include:
Director of sales
Music store owner
Regional sales manager

The mechanical aptitude and manual dexterity required for instrument repairers and restorers is also required for:

Computer repairer      Office machine repairer
Electronic home entertainment      Power tool repairer
   equipment repairer      Vending machine servicer
Home appliance repairer         and repairer

## WORKING CONDITIONS

Most brass, woodwind, string, and percussion instrument repairers work in repair shops or music stores. Piano and organ repairers and tuners usually work on instruments in homes, churches, schools, and may spend several hours a day commuting. Salaried repairers and tuners work out of a shop or store; the self-employed generally work out of their homes. Any of these workers may be required to purchase their own tools that are required to perform this type of work.

Work weeks may be in excess of forty hours. Usually the pace is a busy one, particularly during the peak fall and winter months. This is especially important to those workers who are paid by the piece.

## TRAINING AND QUALIFICATIONS

Though college degrees may or may not specifically be named as requirements for careers in sales or repair of musical equipment, those who have one are decidedly more marketable than those who do not. The benefits derived from a college education cannot be underestimated. For one thing, it provides you with a broad base of knowledge, which is so important when dealing one-on-one with the public on a daily basis. It allows you to speak intelligently about a broad cross section of topics. Well-developed communication skills are another asset you bring with you—so important in being successful in any sales position or a position in music repair. Skills in marketing, sales, finance, music merchandising, and basic math skills are all a plus. You must be able to gain the client's confidence, and the best way to do that is to present a confident, intelligent, well-rounded personality.

A typical community college two-year Associate of Arts (AA) degree designed to focus on sales and business would include the following:

Introduction to accounting

Income tax accounting

Cost accounting

Retailing

Selling

Business law

Introduction to computers

Data processing

Small business management

Insurance

Business communications

Warehouse operations

Those who continue their education, enrolling in a four-year college program might expect to take the following courses:

Principles of marketing

Promotion

Personal selling

Sales forecasting

Marketing research

Sales management

Principles of retailing

Business ownership

Additional valuable courses include:

Advertising

Business management and merchandising

Computer technology

Music history

Marketing

Music appreciation

Music—performing (piano or any other instrument)

Music education

Electronics and sound technology

Piano tuning

It is even possible to find college curriculums designed to focus on music business. Typical courses would include:

Solo instrument

Public performance

Communications

Business psychology

Industrial management

Money and banking

In addition to acquiring sufficient education and training, salespeople should also be articulate, self-confident, enthusiastic, accurate, diplomatic, reliable, organized, persistent, ambitious, aggressive, and detailed-minded. They should also be able to withstand rejection and the pressure to meet sales quotas.

Those interested in acquiring the training that will prepare them to tune pianos should check out various training possibilities. One of the best courses to take is the one endorsed by the Piano Technicians' Guild. The programs last two to three years. A small number of technical schools and colleges offer courses in piano technology or brass, woodwind, string, and electronic musical instrument repair. A few music repair schools offer one- or two-year courses. There are also home-study (correspondence school) courses in piano technology. Graduates of these courses generally refine their skills by working for a time with an experienced tuner or technician.

To be successful as a piano tuner, individuals must have a great interest in the piano, have a good musical "ear," a deep knowledge of the instrument and how it operates, and the ability to play it well. Patience is also important.

Those who work as instrument repairers usually pursue the following progression in skill and career level: trainee, apprentice, repairer/restorer, master. A background in woodworking is helpful. Courses include buffing, dent removal, plating, soldering, small business practices, acoustics, machine tool operation, and on-the-job training for piano and instruments.

Other requirements include good manual dexterity, patience, the ability to deal with the public, knowledge of woodworking, mechanical aptitude, a neat appearance, a pleasant, cooperative manner, attention to detail, a love of music and fine instruments, the ability to distinguish musical pitch, and mechanical abilities.

Musical instrument repairers keep up with developments in their fields by studying trade magazines and manufacturers' service manuals. The Piano Technicians Guild helps its members improve their skills through training conducted at local chapter meetings and at regional and national seminars. Guild members also can take a series of tests to earn the title Registered Piano Technician. The National Association of Professional Band Instrument Repair Technicians offers a similar program, scholarships, and a trade publication. Its members specialize in the repair of woodwind, brass, string, and percussion instruments.

Repairers and technicians who work for large dealers, repair shops, or manufacturers can advance to supervisory positions or go into business for themselves.

## E ARNINGS

Earnings for those in music sales may range from $18,000 to $45,000 for manufacturer's representatives. Music shop sales clerks might expect to average $12,000 to $25,000 and up per year ($30,000 to $50,000 for larger instruments such as pianos and stereo systems). Managers can expect to earn from $20,000 to $50,000 and up per year. Some will receive commissions and bonuses based upon yearly store sales figures.

According to the limited information available, repairers and tuners employed full time by retail music stores average about $26,550. Repairers and tuners who work full time plus supervise at least one other technician average about $34,250. A piano tuner technician working in a piano factory can earn between $12,000 and $40,000 plus per year. Independent piano tuner technicians working full time can earn $25,000 annually.

---

**Average salaries include:**
Apprentice: $8,600 to $10,000 per year
Experienced: $25,000 to $42,000 per year
Repairer/Restorer: $16,000 to $20,000 per year

Many who do this are self-employed, so earnings will vary according to that and geographical area and, of course, the abilities of the professional. Usually self-employed workers can make more money than those working for a store or manufacturer; however, the work may be sporadic, and benefits such as health insurance, holiday and sick pay, and vacations are not provided for you.

Contracts may be arranged between an individual and a music group, conservatory, university, or studio. The individual would then be responsible for all upkeep on the pianos.

## CAREER OUTLOOK

Companies and stores are always looking for good, experienced salespeople at both the wholesale and retail levels. Opportunities will continue to be particularly good for those who have gained experience and display a proven track record.

Musical instrument repairer and tuner jobs are expected to increase about as fast as the average for all occupations through the year 2005. Replacement needs will provide the most job opportunities as many repairers and tuners near retirement age. Several competing factors are expected to influence the demand for musical instrument repairers and tuners. Although the number of people employed as musicians will increase, the number of students of all ages playing musical instruments is expected to grow slowly. Yet consumers should continue to buy more expensive instruments, so they should be willing to spend more on tuning and repairs to protect their value.

## STRATEGY FOR FINDING THE JOBS

### Walk Right In

Sales positions may be acquired on a part-time (or full-time) basis while still in school or afterwards. It may just be a matter of walking in and presenting yourself with a positive appearance and pleasing manner. Bring along a resume and make sure you are prepared to fill out an application (have information at hand such as references, educational information, previous work information, etc.) Any experience in sales will certainly provide you with a quicker entry to a full-time position. Ask for an interview. If they don't give you a date, let them know when you will be calling to follow up on this matter.

### Make Contact by Mail, Phone, or E-Mail

Many music stores, particularly those who sell CDs and tapes and television and stereo equipment are operated by major corporations who often have multiple retail outlets. If they have central management offices, this is a good place to contact. Department stores also usually have music departments who employ people for sales and management positions.

To locate a position as an industry representative, contact a field office of a major record label. Send a resume and cover letter. Address it to the National Sales Director if you cannot obtain the name of the person who would be doing the hiring. Any previous sales experience is a definite plus so be sure to list all that you have. The basic approach to sales is universal no matter what product or service you will be selling.

## Study the Newspapers

Check the want ads. Ask around. Look for signs in windows. Seek out the help of employment agencies.

## Advertise

If you are looking to increase your business, which consists of repairing instruments or tuning or repairing pianos, put up notices in music shops, on supermarket and library posting boards, and in music schools (ask to be recommended).

# PROFESSIONAL ASSOCIATIONS

**Guitar and Accessories Music Marketing Association (GAMMA)**
38-44 West Twenty-first Street
New York, NY 10010

**National Association of Professional Band Instrument Repair Technicians**
P.O. Box 51
Normal, IL 61761

**Piano Technicians Guild**
3930 Washington Street
Kansas City, MO 64111

# CHAPTER SIXTEEN

# PATH 7: OTHER MUSIC CAREERS

*If music be the food of love,*
*play on;*
*Give me excess of it, that,*
*surfeiting,*
*The appetite may sicken,*
*and so die.*

**Shakespeare, *Twelfth Night***

dd the careers in this chapter to your arsenal of possible occupations for music majors.

## DEFINITION OF THE CAREER PATH

If you have a talent for writing or a voracious appetite for viewing and evaluating music events or delight in the thought of cataloguing musical materials or enjoy the prospect of helping others who are facing obstacles, here are some additional occupations in the music industry.

### Music Librarian

A music librarian is able to combine two distinct areas of expertise: an extensive knowledge of all types of music along with skills as a librarian. Music librarians are responsible for the cataloging of all types of musical materials such as tapes, CDs, books, or other media.

# Possible Employers

Music librarians may work at schools, public libraries, private libraries, colleges and universities, music research libraries, conservatories, radio and television stations, orchestras, sheet music or record stores, and other educational locations.

# Training and Qualifications

Situations will vary—in some cases, degrees in both music and library science will be required. In other cases, perhaps a degree in only one or the other will be mandated. For positions in larger institutions, master's degrees in one or both are usually required.

Personal skills required include good organization and memory skills, the ability to get along well with a variety of people, a keen interest and understanding of all types of music, books, and recordings, and usually some knowledge of foreign languages.

# Earnings

Salaries may vary considerably according to the location and scope of the position. The following are sample figures:

Orchestra: $23,000 per year
Educational setting (starting): $12,000 per year
Educational setting (experienced): $27,000 per year
Mid-sized radio station (starting): $13,000 per year
Larger radio station (starting): $15,000 to $19,000 per year

# Career Outlook

Competition is considerable in this field. Those with greater educational credentials will have a better chance for employment. The most likely place to try is a mid-sized radio station.

## Strategy for Finding the Jobs

Working with college human resources departments is always a good idea. Other possibilities would be to contact a music library association for publications that may list available positions. Directly contacting schools, libraries, and music or record stores is another possibility.

## Professional Associations

**Music Library Association**
P.O. Box 487
Canton, MA 02021-0487

### Music Critic

Critics, in general, can seriously affect whether or not a musical concert or other type of musical event will meet with real success—financial and otherwise. Music critics are assigned the responsibility of viewing shows, concerts, or artists' appearances, and writing their opinions of the performance. Some also review CDs and other musical products.

## Possible Employers

Newspapers, magazines, and other forms of communication may employ music critics. To begin, contact a local publication and ask them if you can review a musical event (even if you won't get paid for it). You need to begin to build "clips" (published articles). This is the way you will be able to work your way up to a paying position, larger newspaper, magazine, or other type of publication.

Don't expect this to be a nine-to-five job. Music critics may work evening and weekend hours and be faced with stringent deadlines.

## Training and Qualifications

Usually, magazines and newspapers will require an undergraduate degree with course work in writing, journalism, and communications. Excellent writing skills will need to be demonstrated as well as a solid knowledge of the type of music being critiqued.

As is the case with all writers, critics need the ability to work under pressure with constant deadlines looming. Self-motivation, discipline, objective reporting skills, and a strong background in music are all requirements for this job.

## EARNINGS

Though earnings will vary according to the location of the job, the following represent average salaries:

Local newspaper, writing reviews: $15,000 minimum per year
Local newspaper, with experience: $20,000 to $25,000 per year
Major publication: $17,500 to $100,000 per year

## PROFESSIONAL ASSOCIATIONS

**Music Critics Association (MCA)**
6201 Tuckerman Lane
Rockville, MD 20852

## CAREER OUTLOOK

It is fairly easy to do this kind of work on a part-time basis and difficult to find positions on a full-time basis.

### Music Therapist

All creative therapists (art, drama, music) treat and strive to rehabilitate people with physical, mental, or emotional illnesses or disabilities. In doing so, they work as a team member along with doctors, physical therapists, nurses, psychologists, and psychiatrists.

Music therapists are professionals who develop and direct musical activities and lessons aimed at achieving goals such as improving a patient's level of self-confidence and self-awareness, the relief of depression, or improving physical dexterity. Often the music itself provides an avenue for the patient to express previously unspoken feelings.

## POSSIBLE EMPLOYERS

Many music therapists are assigned to clinics, rehabilitation centers, schools, nursing homes, and hospitals. Some therapists may be affiliated with several establishments at the same time. A number are self-employed and work with patients in their own studios, building a caseload of patients through referrals and consultations with other medical personnel.

## WORKING CONDITIONS

Theoretically, this is a forty-hour week position. However, additional hours may be required. Sometimes a "working service contract" with various facilities is maintained and individuals must work when called upon to fulfill these binding agreements. In these cases, the therapists may work on a one-to-one basis or in a group setting depending on the patient and his or her needs.

## TRAINING AND QUALIFICATIONS

Although required credentials may vary, usually an undergraduate degree in music therapy is a minimum for all music therapists. A master's degree along with course work in music theory, voice studies, instrumental lessons, physiology, psychology, sociology, and biology may be mandatory. National or state certification, requiring paid work experience and a clinical internship (usually six months), is also usually required. Professionals who wish to work in a public school setting must obtain educational certifications in that state.

Music therapists must be understanding, caring, and compassionate. They must have a strong desire and ability to help others. Additionally, they must have excellent musical skills including the ability to play piano and/or guitar and a strong knowledge of music in general.

## EARNINGS

Though salaries vary according to where you are working, the following represent average figures. Most positions also offer benefits such as health insurance, pension plans, and holiday and vacation pay:

Starting: $20,000 to $30,000 per year
Experienced: $25,000 to $30,000 per year in a larger facility or
   institution
Government affiliated: $27,500 to $50,000 per year
Supervisory: $38,000 per year minimum
Government (GS-13 level): $27,000 to $50,000

## CAREER OUTLOOK

This field is one that is relatively new and expanding. Health care facilities continue to grow with time. However, the positions will continue to be difficult to come by, especially full-time positions.

## STRATEGY FOR FINDING THE JOBS

Avenues are available through college and university employment centers, trade publication want ads, newspaper want ads, and associations such as the American Association for Music Therapy (AAMT) or the National Association for Music Therapy, Inc. (NAMT).

## PROFESSIONAL ASSOCIATIONS

**American Association for Music Therapy (AAMT)**
P.O. Box 27177
Philadelphia, PA 19118

**National Association for Music Therapy (NAMT)**
505 Eleventh Street S.E.
Washington, DC 20003

## Music Journalist

Music journalists may start out as staff members at local circulation newspapers. In this capacity, they may author daily, biweekly, or weekly columns about whatever is going on in the world of music. They may also write critiques for musical occasions like concerts, shows, or other music-related events, and may also write reviews of new music products.

Interviews are often a part of what is needed to write articles, so music journalists must be adept in this area. Other skills include researching and the ability to work well with all kinds of people.

After gaining experience, music journalists may be qualified to find positions at larger publications or adopt a specialty such as classical reviewer.

## POSSIBLE JOB TITLES

| | |
|---|---|
| Music critic | Stringer |
| Musical reviewer | Writer |
| Reporter | |

## POSSIBLE EMPLOYERS

When just starting out, smaller publications are possibilities. Once established, opportunities exist in larger cities like New York or Los Angeles, which have major music publications. Obtain a list of all the publications in your area and approach them directly with an effective resume and cover letter.

## RELATED OCCUPATIONS

| | |
|---|---|
| Business writer | Novelist |
| Educational writer | Proposal writer |
| Fiction writer | Restaurant critic |
| Freelance writer | Salesperson |
| Grant writer | Teacher |
| Music publisher | Technical writer |
| Nonfiction writer | |

## WORKING CONDITIONS

Music journalists usually have a desk or office at the publication where they work. Their schedule may be quite erratic since musical events may be presented late at night or on weekends. Added to this is the possibility that there may be little time between the event and the article deadline, producing time constraints and corresponding stress.

## TRAINING AND QUALIFICATIONS

A college degree, preferably in journalism, is generally required. Demonstrated expertise in writing is necessary along with proven experience through published clips or other writing-related experience.

## EARNINGS

Salaries can vary widely. New journalists can expect to earn $15,000 to $20,000 per year. With more experience, yearly figures elevate to $20,000 to $30,000. Established journalists at larger publications can make $50,000 per year.

## CAREER OUTLOOK

The career outlook is cautious but possible for those willing to work their way up from entry-level positions.

## STRATEGY FOR FINDING THE JOBS

Taking any kind of job at a publication (even in a nonwriting capacity or on a part-time basis) may well be worth your while to get your foot in the door. Once people know you and the caliber of work you produce, they often have much more confidence in your abilities. Even offering to write for free provides you with good experience, published clips, and evidence of your eagerness to enter the field. Contact an editor in your local area and offer to do this.

## PROFESSIONAL ASSOCIATIONS

**American Society of Journalists and Authors, Inc.**
1501 Broadway, Suite 302
New York, NY 10036

**International Women's Writing Guild**
Box 810
Gracie Station
New York, NY 10028

**National Writers Association**
1450 South Havana, Suite 424
Aurora, CO 80012

---

### MEET CARLA DeSANTIS

Carla DeSantis took courses at a number of colleges—changing majors from theater arts to journalism to music composition to mass communications. After twenty years as a professional musician, she found a career that combines all of her past majors. She founded *ROCKRGRL Magazine* in January 1995 and serves as Publisher/Editor-in-Chief.

"I had been a professional musician for many years," says Carla. "A few years ago, after getting a computer and meeting many women online who were also musicians, I began to see that most of us had very similar horror stories about the industry. And none of us were aware of the common threads that persisted in all our careers that were a direct result of our being female. For example, I've always been ignored by the male salesclerks at music stores in the past when I was shopping for gear. I was shocked to find out that most women musicians have encountered the same treatment. There are also record labels that will not sign more than a certain number of female acts, and radio stations that will not play more than a certain number of songs by women singers per hour. These facts were appalling to me. I came to realize that this blatant sexism, which is actually illegal in most other professions, is a constant in the music business, and especially in rock and roll, where the music tends to be loud and aggressive.

"Also, I am a single mother who was looking for a way to make a living from home. After seeing many music-related magazine covers with women on the front shown inappropriately dressed, I was inspired to take action. So I took matters into my own hands and now I publish a bimonthly magazine that is distributed internationally and well-known and respected throughout the industry. Ironically, I've been able to attract writers from many of the very publications that perpetuate negative attitudes towards women.

"Since I conceived the idea for *ROCKRGRL* in the summer of 1994, I've spent seven days a week and an average of twelve hours a day on the

continued

continued

magazine. I get up at 6 A.M. and try to accomplish what I can before my son wakes up—editing, writing, order fulfillment, whatever. Then I get him to school at 8:30 A.M. and I'm hard at work until he gets home at 4:00 P.M. After dinner at 7:00, I usually put in another four hours until midnight. Other than the writing of some of the articles and the layout, I assign all the stories to writers, edit them when they come in, make sure there are accompanying photos, sell all the ads, deal with subscriber inquiries, put together web site updates, update the subscriber database, send out renewal notices, bring new copies to the stores where it's been consigned, deal with the printer, field media inquiries, etc. It's very hectic, especially doing this alone, but very rewarding.

"Although I always procrastinate on this, I love to do the editing. It's rewarding to take something good and make it better. I also love seeing the magazine come together. I think every issue continues to look better and better, and I'm very proud of the positive reaction it gets from people. I've had a chance to meet all of my favorite rock stars. And it's thrilling to know that something I've done is read all over the world. I get mail from Spain, Australia, England, everywhere.

"The downside is that it is all-consuming. Selling ads requires many, many follow-up phone calls, and with a bimonthly deadline, time seems to slip away, so I find I am not as effective in that area as I'd like to be. Suddenly, a couple of weeks before the ad deadline, I find myself saying, "Gee, I'd better get some cash in here!"

"As far as advice to others, I'd say spend some time getting as much experience as you can. Because desktop publishing has made it very easy to produce a magazine these days, the universe is flooded with music and pop culture magazines. But paper costs are astronomical, and with a deadline-driven business, it's very easy to get in over your head. I had a background in journalism and owned my own public relations firm for two years, so I had a solid business background. I was also a huge music fan, so I learned as much as I could about the world of music and made a name for myself within the industry. Learn from your mistakes and don't be afraid to make them."

# ADDITIONAL RESOURCES

## BOOKS

**(The) Best Towns in America**
Houghton Mifflin Co.
222 Berkeley Street
Boston, MA 02166

**Career Information Center**
MacMillan Publishing Group
866 Third Avenue
New York, NY 10022

**Careers Encyclopedia**
VGM Career Horizons
NTC/Contemporary Publishing Company
4255 West Touhy Avenue
Lincolnwood, IL 60646

**Careers for Music Lovers**
VGM Career Horizons
NTC/Contemporary Publishing Company
4255 West Touhy Avenue
Lincolnwood, IL 60646

**Dictionary of Occupational Titles**
U.S. Department of Labor
Employment and Training Administration
Distributed by Associated Book Publishers, Inc.

P.O. Box 5657
Scottsdale, AZ 86261

### Directory of Directories
Gale Research Inc.
P.O. Box 33477
Detroit, MI 48232

### Effective Answers to Interview Questions (video)
JIST Works, Inc.
720 North Park Avenue
Indianapolis, IN 46202

### (The) Handbook of Private Schools
Porter Sargent Publishers, Inc.
11 Beacon Street, Suite 1400
Boston, MA 02108

### How to Write a Winning Personal Statement for Graduate and Professional School
Peterson's
P.O. Box 2123
Princeton, NJ 08543

### Index of Majors and Graduate Degrees
College Board Publications
P.O. Box 886
New York, NY 10101

### National Center for Education Statistics
*America's Teachers: Profile of a Profession*
U.S. Department of Education
Office of Educational Research and Improvement
Washington, DC 20208

### National Directory of Internships
National Society for Internships and Experiential Education
3509 Haworth Drive, Suite 207
Raleigh, NC 27609

### National Teacher Exam
Educational Testing Service
P.O. Box 6051
Princeton, NJ 08541

*Occupational Outlook Handbook*
*Occupational Outlook Quarterly*
U.S. Department of Labor
Bureau of Labor Statistics
Washington, DC 20212

*Opportunities in Music Careers*
VGM Career Horizons
NTC/Contemporary Publishing Company
4255 West Touhy Avenue
Lincolnwood, IL 60646

*Peterson's Guide to Four-Year Colleges*
*Peterson's Guide to Independent Secondary Schools*
*Peterson's Guide to Two-Year Colleges*
*Peterson's Guide to Graduate Study*
Peterson's Guides
P.O. Box 2123
Princeton, NJ 08543

*What Can I Do With a Major In?*
Abbott Press
P.O. Box 433
Ridgefield, NJ 07657

*Where the Jobs Are: A Comprehensive Directory of 1200 Journals*
    *Listing Career Opportunities*
Garrett Park Press
P.O. Box 190
Garrett Park, MD 20896

# Booking Agencies

**American Concert**
P.O. Box 23599
Nashville, TN 27202

**BSA Presentations**
P.O. Box 1516
Champaign, IL 60824

**Don Walker Productions**
Walker Productions
360 North Michigan Avenue
Chicago, IL 60601

**Entertainment Artists**
819 Eighteenth Avenue, South
Nashville, TN 37203

**Far West Entertainment**
344 NE Northgate Way, No. 225
Seattle, WA 98125

**Good Music Agency**
P.O. Box 437
Excelsior, MN 55331

**Harmony Artists, Inc.**
8833 Sunset Boulevard
Los Angeles, CA 90069

**International Talent Group**
729 Seventh Avenue
New York, NY 10019

**Long Distance Entertainment**
6801 Hamilton Avenue
Cincinnati, OH 45224

**Miracle Concerts**
10 George Street
Wallingford, CT 06492

**Nationwide Entertainment Services**
7770 Regents Road
San Diego, CA 92122

**Overland Entertainment**
257 West 52nd Street
New York, NY 10019

**Premier Talent**
3 East 54th Street
New York, NY 10022

**Roadstar Productions**
3100 South Lamar
Austin, TX 78704

**Sutton Artists Corp.**
20 West Park Avenue, Suite 305
Long Beach, NY 11561

**The Talent Agency**
1005–A Lavergne Circle
Hendersonville, TN 37075

**Universal Attractions**
225 West 57th Street
New York, NY 10019

**Variety**
15490 Ventura Boulevard
Sherman Oaks, CA 91423

**William Morris Agency**
1350 Avenue of the Americas
New York, NY 10019

# Music Publishers

**Alexis**
P.O. Box 532
Malibu, CA 98265

**Better Times Pubishing**
1203 Biltmore Avenue
High Point, NC 27260

**Camex Music**
535 Fifth Avenue
New York, NY 10017

**DRG Music**
130 West 54th Street
New York, NY 10019

**Fantasy, Inc.**
2600 Tenth Street
Berkeley, CA 94710

**Gatlin Bros. Music, Inc.**
31 Music Square West
Nashville, TN 37229

**Harmony Street Music**
Box 4107
Kansas City, KS 66104

**Joy Jay Publishing**
35 NE 62nd Street
Miami, FL 33138

**Lowery Group**
3051 Clairmont Road, NE
Atlanta, GA 30329

**Miracle Mile Music**
P.O. Box 35449
Los Angeles, CA 90035

**Opryland Music Group, Inc.**
65 Music Square West
Nashville, TN 37015

**Peermusic**
8159 Hollywood Boulevard
Los Angeles, CA 90069

**RCA Music Publishing**
1540 Broadway
New York, NY 10036

**Star International, Inc.**
P.O. Box 470346
Tulsa, OK 74147

**Tillis Tunes**
809 Eighteenth Avenue South
Nashville, TN 37203

**Walt Disney Music Company**
3900 West Alameda Avenue
Burbank, CA 91505

# OTHER PUBLICATIONS

*Musician Magazine*

***The Musician's Guide to Touring and Promotion***
Published by *Musician Magazine* (Yearly)
Provides information on:

Talent buyers

Clubs

Music press

Record labels

Radio

Record stores

Instrument rental/repair

Extensive directories:

Major label A and R

Music conferences

Showcases

Music industry web sites

Tape/disc manufacturers

# INDEX